THE PRINCIPLES OF DEBBIE & GOLIATH

CREATED BY MULTI #1
INTERNATIONAL BEST-SELLING
AUTHOR & AWARD WINNING
SPEAKER ON HABITS

ERIK SWANSON

THE **PRINCIPLES** OF
DEBBIE & GOLIATH

#1 BESTSELLER

FOCUS & ALIGNMENT
Featuring Doria Cordova

Copyright © 2024
THE PRINCIPLES OF DEBBIE & GOLIATH

Manufactured and printed in the United States of America and distributed globally by Integrity Publishing.

Library of Congress Control Number:
Hardback ISBN: 978-1-964330-08-2
Paperback ISBN: 978-1-964330-07-5

Legal Disclaimer & Acknowledgment

The contents of *The Principles of Debbie And Goliath* book series includes various stories, reflections, and experiences by each of our co-authors. It is important to clarify that the views, stories, principles, and opinions expressed by the individual authors in this series are solely their own and do not necessarily reflect the beliefs, policies, or positions of Habitude Warrior International LLC, Integrity Publishing, or their affiliates and partners, or the other individual authors and writers in this series.

Each chapter is the original work of its respective author. While Habitude Warrior International LLC and Integrity Publishing own the copyright rights to the content within this book series, the statements, claims, and backgrounds presented by each contributing author are their sole responsibility. These authors assert that their contributions are their original work and words, and they are accountable for the truthfulness and accuracy of their content.

The diverse collection of stories, examples, and ideas presented in this series aims to offer insights and guidance for overcoming challenges. However, readers are reminded that these narratives are based on the authors' personal experiences and perspectives. As such, not every belief or approach may resonate with or be applicable to all readers. The variety of viewpoints is intended to provide a broad spectrum of experiences and reflections, fostering a rich and diverse dialogue on the subject of empowerment and personal growth.

Furthermore, Habitude Warrior International LLC and Integrity Publishing do not guarantee any specific outcomes or results from applying the principles and strategies outlined in this series. The organizations are not liable for any consequences or effects that may arise from the application of information contained in these books. Readers are encouraged to use their discretion and judgment in interpreting and applying the ideas shared by the co-authors.

~ Habitude Warrior International LLC & Integrity Publishing

CONTENTS

Global Speakers Mastermind & Habitude Warrior Masterminds

Join us and become a member of our tribe! Our Global Speakers Mastermind is a virtual group of amazing thinkers and leaders who meet twice a month. Sessions are designed to be 'to the point' and focused while sharing fantastic techniques to grow your mindset as well as your pocketbooks. We also include famous guest speaker spots for our private Masterclasses. We also designate certain sessions for our members to mastermind with each other & and counsel on the topics discussed in our previous Masterclasses. It's time for you to join a tribe who truly cares about **YOU** and your future and start surrounding yourself with the famous leaders and mentors of our time. It is time for you to up-level your life, businesses, and relationships.

For more information to check out our Masterminds:
Team@HabitudeWarrior.com
www.DecideTobeAwesome.com

10

BECOME AN INTERNATIONAL
#1 BESTSELLING AUTHOR & SPEAKER

Habitude Warrior International has been highlighting award-winning Speakers and #1 Bestselling Authors for over 25 years. They know what it takes to become #1 in your field and how to get the best exposure around the world. If you have ever considered giving yourself the GIFT of becoming a well-known Speaker and a fantastically well known #1 Best-Selling Author, then you should email their team right away to find out more information in how you can become involved. They have the best of the best when it comes to resources in achieving the bestselling status in your particular field. Start surrounding yourself with the N.Y. Times Bestsellers of our time and start seeing your dreams become reality!

For more information to become a #1 Bestselling Author & Speaker on our Habitude Warrior Conferences
Please text the word AUTHORS to 619-304-6268
And also go to:
www.DecideToBeAwesome.com

DEDICATION

BRINGING AWARENESS TO FEMALE FINANCIAL LITERACY

We strive to raise awareness of issues prevalent in our world today. Our goal is to assist in identifying these issues so that we can collectively come together to eradicate them. Our second book in *The Principles of Debbie & Goliath* series is dedicated to the awareness of Female Financial Literacy.

Financial literacy is understanding and effectively using various financial skills, including personal financial management, budgeting, and investing. It is crucial for women to have the knowledge and resources to achieve financial independence and security.

Female financial literacy is essential for empowering women to make informed financial decisions, ultimately leading to improved economic stability and independence. Despite progress in many areas, women still face unique challenges in the financial realm, including the gender pay gap, lower lifetime earnings along with a typically longer life expectancy.

Key topics and principles of female financial literacy include:

Budgeting and Saving: Effective budgeting and saving are foundational skills for financial health. Understanding how to create and stick to a budget, manage expenses, and save for future goals is critical for financial independence.

Investing: Investing is a powerful tool for building wealth over time. Women should be educated about various investment options, the importance of diversification, and strategies for long-term growth.

Debt Management: Understanding how to manage and reduce debt is essential for financial stability. This includes knowledge about different types of debt, interest rates, and repayment strategies. An important is a man is not a plan.

Retirement Planning: Women need to plan for retirement, considering factors like longer life expectancy and potential career breaks. Knowledge about retirement accounts, Social Security benefits, and investment strategies is vital for a secure retirement.

Financial Education and Resources: Access to reliable financial education and resources is crucial for ongoing financial literacy. Utilizing available tools and seeking guidance from financial professionals can help women make informed decisions.

We have amazing support and relationships with female financial resources that provide invaluable knowledge and tools for women everywhere. We want to highlight some of these resources:

Money & You® Worldwide by Dame Doria Cordova: A comprehensive program that provides practical financial education and tools for achieving financial success and independence.

***Think and Grow Rich for Women* by Sharon Lechter:** This book is a great resource offering timeless financial principles tailored specifically for women, providing inspiration and strategies for financial growth.

***The Millionaire Maker* by Loral Langemeier:** Learn how to act, think, and make money as the wealthy do and uncover your financial personality.

It's important to note that financial literacy can positively impact all areas of life, contributing to overall well-being and empowerment. Women can achieve greater independence, security, and confidence by becoming financially literate.

If you or someone you know is seeking to improve their financial literacy, there are numerous resources available. We've listed some in the back of this book for you.

Remember, taking control of your financial future is a powerful step towards empowerment and independence.

For a list of resources, please turn to page 245.

INTRODUCTION

THE PRINCIPLES OF DEBBIE & GOLIATH

In the heart of every woman lies a story of resilience, a tale of overcoming, and a triumph of success... much like the story of David and Goliath. Yet, in our modern world, the challenges faced are often more nuanced, complex, and deeply intertwined with the fabric of societal expectations and personal struggles. *The Principles of Debbie and Goliath* book series is a beacon of hope and female empowerment, designed to guide and inspire women of all ages.

This series is a unique compilation of wisdom, experiences, and strategies from various women, including celebrities and thought leaders, each sharing their insights to uplift and empower. Each volume in this series is dedicated to a specific theme, resonating with the different stages of a woman's journey towards self-awareness and empowerment.

This series is unique in that it is 100% female empowered and co-authored. Each of the three books in the series will include 33 female Co-Authors and one female Celebrity Author. Each author teaches principles on how to conquer obstacles in life and how to handle them for ultimate success to become a truly global empowered female. Each Co-Author's chapter focuses on the perspective of giving their younger female 13-year-old self advice, suggestions, and counsel to become an empowered female leader in life, and is sure to become a blueprint for the female teenager's success journey around the globe! Our goal is to empower females and empower our world in beautiful harmony.

Volume 1: Habits of Success

In our first volume, we delve into the 'Habits of Success.' This book is a treasure trove of practical advice and motivational stories, focusing on developing a strong sense of self, cultivating resilience, and fostering a mindset geared towards success. From navigating self-confidence issues to mastering financial literacy, this volume is designed to equip female readers with the habits and tools necessary to create a foundation of personal female empowerment.

Volume 2: Focus & Alignment

The second volume, 'Focus & Alignment,' shifts the lens to the importance of aligning one's values, goals, and actions. Here, we explore the art of maintaining focus amidst life's myriad challenges. This volume tackles topics such as dealing with relationship dynamics, understanding situational awareness, and overcoming societal pressures, all crucial for aligning our female reader's inner compass towards personal and professional fulfillment.

Volume 3: Global Female Empowerment

In our final volume in this series, 'Global Female Empowerment,' the narrative extends beyond individual struggles, addressing issues that impact females on a global scale. This book is an homage to the collective power of women, discussing habits and strategies to allow our young female readers to not have to reinvent the wheel, but to learn from our Co-Author's experiences. It's a call to action for women to unite in their diversity, strength, and resilience to effect positive change in the world.

The Principles of Debbie and Goliath is more than a book series; it's a female movement! It's a conversation between generations—from the Co-Authors to their 13-year-old selves. Each story in the series shares principles toward understanding and overcoming the unique challenges that women face in today's society. Join us on this empowering journey, and discover how to turn your challenges into stepping stones for success.

ERIK SWANSON

Multi #1 Best-Selling Author, International Award Winning Speaker, Creator of *The Principles of Debbie & Goliath*, Founder of Habitude Warrior International and Integrity Publishing

Success isn't about how much money you make; it's about the difference you make in people's lives.

~ Michelle Obama

DAME DORIA (DC) CORDOVA

FOCUS & ALIGNMENT— ATTAINED BY OUR SUBCONSCIOUS

I am so honored to share the principles of focus and alignment, which are ultimately guided by the "greatest power" for any human being: the Subconscious. It's a privilege to write and share what I've learned in nearly five decades of working on myself.

Once we understand the potential benefits and drawbacks of the Subconscious and have established firewalls and self-mastery tools to deal with it under any adverse circumstance, our confidence, self-trust, and self-mastery go through the roof!

I know that I can support you in having greater success, personal power, prosperity, health, peace, and joy. I can help you to have a life where you can live in the greatest experience of them all: Sufficiency!

The Subconscious mind has been a topic of fascination and debate for centuries. It is widely known that our Subconscious thoughts and emotions play a significant role in shaping our decisions and relationships, especially in the business world… Everywhere we look!

Bottom line: The Subconscious has a huge influence on our lives. Allow me to offer practical guidance on overcoming these pitfalls, fostering greater conscious awareness, and enhancing the overall quality of important decisions.

Let me share a bit about my life to give you a little context as to why I have "earned the right" to speak about this subject. In the late 1970s, through a series of wondrous circumstances that I consciously never imagined, I became part of the team of pioneers of the entrepreneurial, experiential, transformational training industry, which now permeates the industry globally. This field, of course, supports people around the world in clearing their Subconscious and reaching the life of their dreams.

Everyone's life is affected by Generalized Principles. A Generalized Principle is always true. These are principles proven by science and physics. Whether we believe in them or not, they exist. One Generalized Principle is gravity; another is leverage; and one not so well-known but equally powerful is precession. Precession is the physics term for ripple effects. They are always present.

The synergy that can be created when we understand how powerfully the Subconscious affects our thoughts, behaviors, feelings, and actions, and learn to manage it, is extraordinary.

At the young age of 26, through a spiritual awakening and having attended one of the first (and most successful) human potential training, EST, I was blessed to learn at the time that if I couldn't have control over my circumstances (I had experienced the tremendous loss of my beloved, two miscarriages, and a dozen friends), at least I could have control of my consciousness.

I finally had a glimpse that I could have a life that could work for me with much less fear, anxiety, and stress... The possibilities were heavenly! I knew I could be financially successful. I just didn't know that I could also be personally happy and live a purpose-driven life.

Once I started putting my attention on clearing my Subconscious of negative programming, my life pivoted to what eventually led me to create the results that are evident today.

There wasn't as much research in the 1970s as there is now. We now know that self-mastery work, exercise, breathing, healthy foods, a focus on adding value to others, being loving and kind, having integrity, and committing our lives to the betterment of humanity can bring us true happiness and joy.

As a Latina woman who accomplished the "American dream," I know that it had much to do with the values that were taught to me by my mother, auntie, grandmother, and other amazing family members who led my thinking.

And then there was the Subconscious…

I had to overcome strong beliefs, thoughts, and decisions that I had made because of my environment, as I had been literally "brainwashed" in traditional schools (as had everyone else). I had to learn Financial Literacy on my own by attending programs like the *Burklyn Business School* (which evolved into what I own today, the *Excellerated Business Schools and Money & You programs*) and other *Excellerated* programs taught by experts outside of traditional education.

I had to clear Subconscious blocks to achieve the level of success that I knew I had in me, and thank God, I realized that I actually had to raise my "deservability" level in order to allow more success, in every area of my life.

How did I do that? First, I am eternally thankful to Sondra Ray, one of the original metaphysicians who influenced many of the leaders in the industry, including myself. When I discovered that I wanted to commit myself to the betterment of humanity and attended the first business school for entrepreneurs of its kind that I mentioned earlier, all these negative thoughts began to literally spurt from my Subconscious. I found myself fighting beliefs that I didn't know I had.

She then introduced me to the *"Magical Exercises"* (a title that emerged after decades of personally using them, as many other leaders in our industry). I had to clear my Subconscious of the beliefs about money, business, and success that I had learned from my parents, family, school, church, books, movies, the environment—essentially, the world!

Most of humanity is programmed to believe that we live in a world of scarcity—even though the Malthusian theory of economics (the work of governments is to manage scarce resources) was proven obsolete in the early 1970s. Think about that… That was over 50 years ago! It was proven then that the world had enough resources to feed everyone, to house everyone, to have energy to use for refrigeration to be used for medicines and food.

The systems and tools were there to share energy sources for the world to have electricity, which is essential to eradicating poverty and hunger. We actually live in a world that has enough, yet sufficiency is one of the most fleeting experiences for so many!

If you don't believe that, your Subconscious is hard at work. And here's where the daily, moment-to-moment discipline comes into play: take three deep breaths. Feel the reaction, question what is being activated, and decide if (whatever you are feeling) is worth working on so that you are the CEO of your life, and the captain of your ship. This will help you clearly and soberly make decisions that will empower you to have a successful life.

Recognize when you are in reaction. Take three deep breaths and come back to center. Do the work and find that inner family that can lead you to have more courage, more clarity, and more certainty than that which you choose, which will lead you to a better life.

I learned this very young: Just because I don't believe something, doesn't mean that it isn't true. Your beliefs will taint your reality so that you will find the evidence necessary to make those beliefs true. You can actually see it in the division that has been created in the world today around medicine, science, and technology.

Who is running the show, you or your Subconscious? Are you aware of the beliefs that you have about the subject that you are tackling today? Do you have the correct information, facts, and what has worked in that situation? Are you willing to learn from other people's mistakes? Or are you the type that will spend the rest of your life having the same "learning experiences" (mistakes), hoping for a different outcome?

Do the *Magical Exercises* that have made a huge difference to so many who have done them. You can find them in our *FridaysWithDoria.com* global platform under Resources. Clear your Subconscious and do the daily work to create a reality that empowers you, and allows you to find the information, tools, and techniques that have worked for tens of millions to have a successful business, or organization (for-profit or non-profit).

Study those who have created extraordinary results in the area that you are interested in, or already have success in. Remember, money has three stages: making it, keeping it, and growing it. What stage are you in? Each stage requires for your Subconscious to have empowering beliefs every step of the way. It's the greatest power, after all.

If your Subconscious is running amok with beliefs that you have collected unchecked, you will have chaos. If you are aware of them and are CONSCIOUSLY working on them, you will have power.

"It is the way," as they say in the *Mandalorian* – the *Star Wars* offshoot.

Consciously increase your self-awareness. Developing a deeper understanding of your emotions, thoughts, and biases can help you recognize when they might be influencing your decision-making. Mindfulness meditation, journaling, and self-reflection exercises such as the *Magical Exercises* are effective ways to cultivate self-awareness.

I personally have practiced *Transcendental Meditation* (TM) for 15 years without fail. It has been one of my greatest disciplines, and here's why.

Once you begin to have self-mastery, you will find that your intuition (gut feeling) will become more prevalent... Your ability to process new information and experiences will lead you to insights that may not be immediately apparent through logical analysis. Intuition can be a valuable tool in making quick decisions or identifying potential opportunities and risks. My ability to make decisions has sped up and improved.

Your emotional intelligence will increase exponentially. You will find that certain situations that used to trigger you no longer do. Learn to manage your emotions effectively. Acknowledge and validate your emotions but avoid letting them dictate your decisions. Techniques such as emotional intelligence training, stress management, and seeking feedback from trusted mentors, colleagues, and friends can help you regulate your emotions and make more balanced decisions.

You will excel at identifying patterns and connections between seemingly unrelated pieces of information, which can lead to innovative ideas and solutions. You will have enhanced creativity. Many creative insights and ideas arise from the Subconscious mind, often when we least expect them. This can lead to breakthroughs in problem-solving and the development of new products or strategies.

I recommend that you create environments that foster creativity in your business, organization, and family! Encourage brainstorming sessions, open discussions, and collaboration within your teams/family to stimulate the Subconscious mind and generate innovative ideas. Providing a safe space for experimentation and risk-taking can lead to breakthroughs in problem-solving.

Remember, the Subconscious mind wields significant influence over our business decisions and relationships. By understanding its origins and recognizing its potential benefits and drawbacks, we can develop strategies to harness its power and not only make better-informed decisions, but we can also design our lives so that we actualize our most cherished heart's desires and are focused on what we are truly aligned with!

DAME DORIA (DC) CORDOVA, PHD (HON.)

Dame Doria Cordova owns *Excellerated Business Schools® for Entrepreneurs* and *Money & You®*, a global organization with over 200,000 participants since 1979 from over 85 countries, especially from Asia Pacific and the Americas. The programs are taught in English, Chinese, Japanese, Vietnamese, Tamil, and Bahasa – soon expanding to Hindi, and other Indian languages– plus Spanish, and others... Many of today's wealth and business leaders have attended the *Money & You* program and transformed the way they teach and run their organizations.

Through these graduates, including her business partnership of 9 years from 1985 to 1994 with Robert T. Kiyosaki of *Rich Dad/Poor Dad* fame, Dame Cordova's work has touched the lives of millions all over the world. The essence of her work is to not only focus on the bottom line and profits but also to offer products and services that add value to humanity.

She is the only Latin woman who was part of the group of pioneers, led by Marshall Thurber and Bobbi DePorter of *www.Supercamp.com*, who began the development of the transformational, experiential, entrepreneurial training industry. She inherited the work nearly 40 years ago, which has expanded to what it is today through countless partners, associates, teams, graduates, and the support of many.

Along with Robert Kiyosaki, of the *Rich Dad/Poor Dad* series, in 1985, they opened that industry in Australia, New Zealand, and later Singapore. Subsequently, along with new partners, Malaysia, Taiwan, Hong Kong, China, Indonesia, India, Thailand, Philippines, Cambodia, Vietnam, Canada, and other markets have been opened. Their larger market is in the Chinese language — having been in China for over two decades. Dr. Willson Lin and his team have put the programs "on the map." Her latest expansion of the work is the *Money & You: Doria's Distinctions Home Study* program, along with the publication of the *Money & You Book Series*.

www.DoriaCordova.com

ALICIA COURI

DIAMOND IN THE ROUGH

When I was 17 years old, my biggest life goals were to move to America, either to New York City or Miami, study fashion in college, become a fashion buyer, and travel the world. Living on the Island of Trinidad as a teenager with these massive dreams and absolutely no way of even conceiving how it would ever happen, however, was the biggest challenge I faced. But not the only one.

I didn't have the greatest of grades in school, mostly because I really disliked school. Okay, that's not entirely true, I actually really, really hated school; I hated going to class, I hated having my teachers constantly compare me to my older sister who was, in their eyes, just perfect. I hated feeling stupid all the time and being called stupid all the time.

I didn't see any path to college and didn't even know how I was even going to make it out of school successfully, especially when my teachers didn't even think I would successfully finish their class. I just wanted to get through my teen years, move and start a whole new life where everyone didn't think I was stupid.

By the time I was 16, I completed my CXC-O level exams, which is the standard testing in the Caribbean Islands to graduate. To mine and everyone's surprise, I passed. Passing the exam entitled me to either get a job or move on to higher education—A levels if I wanted to. That was an additional 2 years of schooling. I shocked my mom when I told her I wanted to go back to school to complete my A level exams, especially since I barely got through the O levels.

The biggest advantage of doing my A level was that I got an opportunity to change schools and get a fresh new start. I thought, no one here knew me so I can be whoever I want to be. I made the decision to be a very different student than I had been in the past. For most of my school life, I was in the shadow of Leisel, my sister, who was perfect. She was obedient, she did all her work, she loved reading and studied really hard. She was a straight A student who was brilliant at Math, Physics, Sciences, French, Geography, History and pretty much anything she studied.

I, on the other hand, was horrible at math, didn't enjoy reading big thick books, couldn't get French or Spanish, Sciences were my nemesis, and the teachers were not excited to have me in their class. To show how bad things were for me, my French teacher banned me from her class. I was devastated, because at the time, I had fantasies of becoming a lawyer or psychologist and needed French on my transcript. (If I was honest with myself, I would have admitted that those careers were never in my future even on my best day lol.)

I was accepted into St. Georges College, a school that was a big part of my dad's family when he was growing up. I was going to make the family name proud. As I entered my new school, I was determined to sit in the front of class, pay attention and do better. No one knew me so I didn't have that reputation of following after my sister and being the lesser one—the stupid, lazy one that was a quitter.

I didn't sit in the back where I could hide, talk, and not pay attention. I made the decision to focus and become a better student. I was ready to be the A student I hadn't been since elementary school.

Then I stepped into my English literature class....

The teacher, Mr. Ragunanan, gave us the rules of the class. He was strict and made sure he told us that he never gave out A's—Ooof, I felt discouraged because, for the first time in my life, I thought I could finally study hard and get A's in my class and here, on the first day, my teacher said he wasn't going to give us an A. But then he continued, "I never give out A's unless they are well deserved."

There was hope....

I was determined to at least get B's in his class because, in my mind, that would be like an A grade. Mr. Ragunanan was one of my best teachers. He taught me to love literature. He believed in me, he challenged me, and I felt safe asking questions when I didn't understand. He wasn't an ogre like everyone thought when they called him names behind his back. Lots of students that had him called him so many different names, but that's because he challenged them to be better.

I understood why they called him names: I used to be like that back in my previous school, I called mean teachers names, and was afraid to ask questions and be called stupid. But even though Rags was tough (yes, we called him Rags as a term of endearment), he wanted us to learn, especially by asking questions when you don't know because that was the only way to learn.

As we went through the year, we tackled one of the most difficult pieces of literature, Chaucer and the Canterbury Tales, written in ye ole English. Just understanding what the characters were saying was a challenge and at times got really frustrating, but Mr. Ragunanan made it so fascinating and enjoyable.

He made us think. He made us debate. He made us love Chaucer. For the first time, I felt really successful in school and not a failure. He even had us over to his house to celebrate the end of a great year for all of us in his class.

From as early as I can remember, I had challenges in school. Numbers and math were very difficult, I also found it challenging when spelling. I didn't know it at the time and was never formally tested but because I transposed numbers and letters, I believe I have a bit of dyslexia coupled with dyscalculia. Math and Sciences were hard because numbers and formulas were just jumbled, and languages were challenging because I

35

mixed up letters, too. As hard as I tried, I couldn't remember formulas, their sequences or how to spell in another language.

In addition, what I learned later in my life was that the way my brain is wired to operate and function was not aligned with the way school and classes are designed. There is a part of the brain that is called Conative. This is where your brain develops the drive to strive and problem solve. The opportunity to explore the conative part of the brain is something I am passionate about sharing with teens and adults to help them, especially if they are struggling to know that they are not broken or stupid but very powerful.

Albert Einstein said, "Everyone is a genius, but if you judge a fish by its ability to climb a tree, it will live it's entire life believing it's stupid."

I understand that quote because I felt like a fish climbing a tree most of my life, until I learned how my brain works. So, if you feel like that fish climbing a tree, reach out to me, and I'd be happy to help you learn your strengths and harness them to put you on track to success.

If I didn't decide to go back to school and take English Literature, I would have never had the opportunity to experience my ability to learn, grow, and thrive.

I realized my dream of moving to Miami and getting my degree in fashion. I had an opportunity to travel the world as a flight attendant, so even if your dream seems impossible now, keep dreaming because if you persevere, you can achieve more than you can even imagine if you continue to believe in yourself.

ALICIA COURI

About Alecia Couri: Alicia Couri, CEO of Audacious Concepts Inc., and founder of RedCarpetCEO™, is a multi-award-winning international & TEDx speaker, a Best-Selling Author, Business consultant and Legacy Queen for Woman of Achievement. She is passionate about empowering women to "own their awesome".

Author's Website: *www.AudaciousConceptsInc.Now.Site*

Book Series Website: *www.ThePrinciplesOfDebbieAndGoliath.com*

AMY KEIDERLING
YOUR INNER STRENGTH

I AM STRONG. I AM POWERFUL. I AM FOCUS. I AM ALIGNMENT. I AM ENOUGH. I AM COLLABORATIVE. I AM RESILIENT. I AM INSPIRING. I AM CARING. I AM PASSIONATE. I AM ME!

I AM BE-U-tiful!

When I reflect on those empowering self-love statements, I am reminded of the journey that led me here. Each affirmation, each word, represents a part of my soul that has been nurtured, challenged, and ultimately empowered through years of growth and self-discovery. It's a journey that continues, and now, it's time to embrace the next chapter of our lives with a focus on two crucial elements: Focus and Alignment.

The Power of Focus

Focus is the ability to center your mind, your efforts, and your heart on what truly matters. It's about filtering out the noise and distractions that life inevitably throws our way and zeroing in on our goals, our dreams, and our passions. When we focus, we are not just aiming for success; we are honing our energy on the things that align with our true purpose.

I remember a time when my life felt like a whirlwind of tasks, responsibilities, and endless to-do lists. It was easy to get lost in the chaos, to feel overwhelmed and unsure of which direction to take. But then, I had a revelation: clarity comes when we prioritize and focus on what is truly important.

The Focus Funnel

Think of your goals and responsibilities as a funnel. At the top, everything pours in—work, family, personal aspirations, social commitments. As these elements move down the funnel, they get filtered and prioritized. Ask yourself these questions:

- What tasks align with my long-term goals?
- Which activities bring me joy and fulfillment?
- What can I delegate or eliminate?

By filtering your tasks through this funnel, you can concentrate your energy on what truly matters, ensuring that your efforts are aligned with your deepest values and aspirations.

Aligning with Purpose

Alignment is about ensuring that your actions, beliefs, and goals are in harmony with your true self. It's about living authentically and making choices that resonate with who you are at your core. When we are aligned, we move through life with a sense of ease and purpose, knowing that we are on the right path.

One of my favorite analogies for alignment comes from my love of vintage cars. Imagine driving a classic car that is out of alignment. It drifts to the side, the ride is rough, and it takes extra effort to stay on course. But when the car is properly aligned, the drive is smooth, and you can enjoy the journey.

The Alignment Check

To ensure your life is in alignment, perform regular "alignment checks:"

1. **Reflect on Your Values:** Are your actions reflecting your core values? If not, what needs to change?

2. **Set Intentional Goals:** Are your goals aligned with your purpose and passions? Reevaluate and adjust as needed.

3. **Listen to Your Inner Voice:** Are you honoring your intuition and inner wisdom? Trust yourself and make decisions that feel right.

Working Together to Achieve Goals

No woman is an island, and one of the most powerful ways to achieve our goals is by working together. Collaboration and support from others can amplify our efforts and help us overcome challenges that seem insurmountable on our own.

In my life, I've had the privilege of working with incredible women who have not only supported me but have also inspired me to reach higher. Together, we've tackled projects, shared dreams, and celebrated successes. It's a reminder that we are stronger together.

Teaching Moment: Building a Support Network

To build a strong support network, consider these steps:

1. **Identify Your Allies:** Who in your life shares your values and goals? Reach out to them and nurture these relationships.

2. **Communicate Openly:** Share your dreams, challenges, and aspirations with your network. Open communication fosters trust and collaboration.

3. **Offer Support:** Be willing to give as much as you receive. Support others in their journeys, and you'll find that they will be there for you when you need it.

Facing Your Goliaths

Life is full of challenges—our Goliaths—that can seem overwhelming and insurmountable. But remember, every Goliath can be defeated when we face it with courage, focus, and alignment.

In my own journey, I've faced numerous Goliaths: self-doubt, fear of failure, and the ever-present challenge of balancing personal and professional life. Each time, I've learned that the key to overcoming these challenges lies in staying true to myself, focusing on my goals, and leaning on my support network.

The Goliath Plan

When facing a Goliath, create a plan:

1. Define the Challenge: Clearly identify what your Goliath is.
2. Break It Down: Divide the challenge into smaller, manageable tasks.
3. Stay Focused: Keep your eye on the goal and stay committed to your plan.
4. Seek Support: Don't be afraid to ask for help and lean on your support network.

Embracing the Journey

As we continue our journey of self-discovery and empowerment, remember that focus and alignment are not destinations but ongoing processes. Embrace the journey with an open heart, a focused mind, and the willingness to align with your true self.

I AM FOCUS. I AM ALIGNMENT. I AM BE-U-tiful!

To all the Wonder-ful Girls out there, remember: You are strong, you are capable, and you are never alone. Embrace your inner Wonder Woman, face your Goliaths with courage, and build a life that is aligned with your deepest dreams and values.

Together, we can achieve greatness. Together, we can overcome any challenge. Together, we can inspire and lift each other up. Remember these daily affirmations and repeat them like a song:

"I AM STRONG. I AM POWERFUL. I AM FOCUS. I AM ALIGNMENT. I AM ENOUGH. I AM COLLABORATIVE. I AM RESILIENT. I AM INSPIRING. I AM CARING. I AM PASSIONATE. I AM ME!
I AM BE-U-tiful!
I AM AMY!
LIFE IS NOW! NOW IT IS YOUR TURN!
"I AM...""

By embracing focus and alignment, and by working together, we can all become the heroes of our own stories. Let's unite on this journey together and create a world where every woman can shine and thrive.

AMY KEIDERLING

About Amy Keiderling: Amy Keiderling is a Rebel Soul Guide. She helps to navigate you to find your soul's purpose. Think of her as a co-pilot on the road of life. When the road gets bumpy, curvy, or just seems full of obstacles and detours, we will pull out our Rebel Roadmap and navigate it together.

Amy Keiderling is the owner of Modville, as well as an adventure guide with Modville Tours. Amy has always been an avid collector of anything vintage; the instant connection a piece gives you to a memory or story is why she loves her fab finds. Amy's passion grew stronger when she met Keith, as his passion for custom vintage cars, motorcycles, and random collectibles grew their collection. When Amy and Keith are not taking adventure lovers on chartered bus vacations or riding around on their motorcycles, you will find them lounging in Modville or out searching for another piece and their story. Amy encourages everyone to find their story, their fab finds, and adventures!

Author's Website: *www.ItsAMoAdventure.com*

Book Series Website: *www.ThePrinciplesofDebbieandGoliath.com*

AZADEH BENNETT

FREEDOM IS NOT FREE

- -

"I would like it that I am going to protest; when a few years have passed, I will be happy that everything has changed because I have protested today."
~ **Hadis Najafi**
(Fatally shot six times while protesting on Sept. 21, 2022, in Iran.)

Goliath is not a myth. It's not just a story character from the Bible. Goliath exists in many forms in our world today. Dictator regimes and oppressive governments are the Goliaths that many people face. In September 2022, the "Woman Life Freedom" movement arose in Iran when the regime killed Mahsa Amini over her hijab. People couldn't stand it anymore and protested against the Islamic regime and its mandatory hijab for women. The government responded by killing more people.

Hadis Najafi, a 22-year-old girl, went to protest and never returned home. She was shot six times in the face, throat, and chest. The regime buried her under strict control, not allowing her family to mourn her properly. They even beat her father and threatened her family to declare that Hadis died of natural causes. Many people in Iran have been killed and are still being executed. The Goliath of oppression gets stronger because it's fed, supported, and backed by other Goliaths worldwide.

My heart goes out to the people and women in Iran who have risen for their freedom and justice against this brutal regime. My mission is to stand with the people in Iran and be their voice in the U.S. and Western countries. This mission led me to envision creating an animation of the epic legendary *Book of Kings* (Shahnameh). I want to introduce it to Western audiences to show where the people of Iran come from and what they are standing for in their lives and their country.

The Significance of Shahnameh: A Beacon of Justice and Freedom

You might ask, what is Shahnameh? I would love to tell you more about this book, its importance, and the reason why I have chosen this book to introduce to the world.

The Shahnameh, or *Book of Kings*, is a monumental piece of Persian literature, written by the poet Ferdowsi around the year 1000. It is one of the world's longest epic poems, telling the rich history, culture, and mythology of Iran from its earliest days until the Islamic conquest. The stories in the Shahnameh are not just historical accounts; they are filled with timeless themes of justice, freedom, and the eternal struggle between good and evil. Through its legendary heroes and rulers, the Shahnameh promotes values like courage, honor, and ethical leadership, resonating with Iranians and people around the world.

The tales of Shahnameh serve as a powerful reminder of the principles of justice and freedom that should guide not only individuals but also governments and rulers. Characters such as Rostam, the mightiest hero of Iranian mythology, and the wise and just King Khosrow, exemplify the virtues of bravery, wisdom, and fairness. These stories highlight the importance of moral integrity and ethical governance. They remind us that true leadership is about serving the people and upholding justice.

In today's world, where oppressive regimes and injustices still exist, the Shahnameh's messages are more relevant than ever, inspiring individuals and leaders to stand up for what is right and to strive for a world where freedom and justice prevail.

These are the reasons why I chose Shahnameh.

My Passion for Freedom and Storytelling

The path I've chosen is driven by two deep callings—standing for freedom alongside the resilient people of Iran, and sharing the empowering stories of the Shahnameh through animation. These dual passions provide the focus and alignment that guide me through challenges and fuel my determination.

Finding My Voice for Justice

Ever since the tragic death of Hadis Najafi, the brave 22-year-old protester fatally shot for demanding basic human rights, I've been gripped by an unshakable drive to amplify the voices of the oppressed in Iran. Witnessing their relentless courage to stand up to the oppressive regime, despite facing modern-day Goliaths, stirred something profound within me.

Staying true to this mission of elevating human dignity isn't easy. I've had to make sacrifices, face criticism, and persevere through daunting obstacles. But my "why"—a world where all people are free to live authentically without fear—keeps me focused and unwavering. This purpose is my guiding light, empowering me to push forward no matter how formidable the challenges seem.

The Power of Ancient Stories

In parallel with this justice work, my creativity has been captured by the ancient Persian tales in the epic Shahnameh. These mythological stories, rich with warriors overcoming battles of good versus evil, deeply resonate with the struggle for freedom Iranians face today. I'm driven to breathe new life into these profound narratives through animation.

Turning the revered Shahnameh into a visual masterpiece is an immense undertaking fraught with creative roadblocks. However, by aligning this artistic ambition with my purpose of elevating virtuous stories that can inspire humanity, I find a reservoir of motivation and persistence. Each frame brings me closer to sharing these empowering cultural legacies with the world.

Collaborating for Impact

On this dual journey, I've been fortunate to connect with incredible individuals and organizations who share my passion for freedom, justice and the preservation of meaningful stories. Our combined skills, perspectives and determination propel our efforts farther than any of us could go alone.

Together, we are conquering creative barriers, amplifying marginalized voices, and spreading a unifying message—that oppression, like the biblical Goliath, will ultimately fall to the courage and moral fortitude of the human spirit. With aligned focus and the power of community, no obstacle is too daunting.

The road ahead won't be easy—there will be many "Goliaths" for me to face. But like Hadis, David, and other pioneers for justice, I have the power to persist with focus and brave determination. My purpose is a beacon that can never be extinguished, lighting the way for me to create the change I wish to see.

My Commitment

If I could share advice with my 14-year-old self, I would say: Never underestimate how your courage today can spark positive change for tomorrow. Discover the callings that set your soul on fire, stay stubbornly committed to them, and find collaborators who share your vision. Life's challenges are inevitable, but your focused passion and moral convictions will give you strength.

To the younger generation, especially young women: identify the change you wish to see in the world and have unwavering faith in your ability to help manifest it. Let your unique gifts, perspectives, and values guide the positive impact only you can create.

My mission of elevating Iran's human rights movement and giving a new voice to uplifting stories may seem lofty. But powered by focus, alignment, and an incredible global community, I'm confident these dreams will become reality. We need not be deterred by modern-day

Goliaths, for it's the courage and moral clarity of our unified "Davids" or in this case unified "Debbies," that will shape a freer, more just world.

The Power of Focus and Alignment: A Message for You

Focus and alignment are essential in conquering challenges and achieving your dreams. They help you stay true to your mission and purpose, guiding you through difficult times and empowering you to overcome obstacles.

Staying True to Your Mission

Focusing on your mission and purpose helps you align your actions with your values. When you know what you stand for and what you want to achieve, it becomes easier to make decisions that keep you on the right path. This alignment keeps you grounded and motivated, even when facing challenges as daunting as Goliath.

Overcoming Challenges

Having a clear mission and purpose provides the strength and determination needed to conquer challenges. Just like Hadis Najafi, who bravely protested for freedom, you can stand up against your own Goliaths. Whether it's a difficult project at school, a personal struggle, or standing up for what you believe in, your mission and purpose give you the courage to persevere.

Collaborating for Success

Working with others who share your mission and values can accelerate your progress. Collaboration brings diverse perspectives, skills, and support, making it easier to achieve your goals. Surround yourself with people who inspire you and help you stay focused on your mission. Together, you can overcome challenges more effectively and create meaningful change.

Focus and alignment are powerful tools that help you navigate through life's challenges and achieve your dreams. By staying true to your mission and purpose, working with others, and staying resilient, you can conquer any Goliath that stands in your way. Remember, your journey may inspire others and create a ripple effect of positive change in the world. Stay focused, stay aligned, and keep moving forward.

AZADEH BENNETT

About Azadeh Bennett: Azadeh Bennett, a dynamic creative leadership consultant and transformational coach, author and speaker, is a fervent advocate for "Woman Life Freedom," tirelessly championing the rights of women globally. Armed with master's degrees in MBA, Strategic Communication, and Global Studies, she is dedicated to empowering individuals on their journey to personal and professional growth.

Azadeh's unwavering dedication is complemented by her loving marriage to Jason Bennett, whose steadfast support fuels her passion for transformation and freedom. Together, they embody the power of love and partnership in pursuing one's life purpose.

Beyond her professional endeavors, Azadeh finds solace in nature through hiking and expresses her creativity by playing the harp, painting with acrylics, and playing with Generative AI. Her commitment to fostering creativity, leadership, freedom, and communication shines through in her work with individuals and organizations.

Moreover, Azadeh is a visionary strategist who excels in connecting people through love and creating joyous experiences. Her remarkable vision to visualize Shahnameh in animation and share it with the world showcases her profound cultural intelligence and communication skills, enriching global understanding and appreciation for Persian culture.

Author's Website: *www.AzadehBennett.com*

Book Series Website: *www.ThePrinciplesOfDebbieAndGoliath.com*

DR. BETTY SPEAKS

GUIDED BY PURPOSE: MENTORING TOMORROW'S LEADERS TODAY

What happens when you combine the strength of military leadership, the wisdom of educational achievement, and the heart of a mentor? You transform lives and build communities that flourish against all odds.

Growing up in a blended family, facing childhood poverty, and enduring bullying encounters were significant challenges that shaped my determination to succeed. These experiences fueled my motivation to rise above adversity and ignited my passion for educating and uplifting others.

Early in my career, I discovered the transformative power of mentorship while working with at-risk children around the world. My purpose became clear: to mentor these young souls and guide their families in essential life skills. One pivotal moment was during a mentorship session with a 10-year-old girl who had lost hope. By focusing on her potential and providing guidance on personal development and financial literacy, I witnessed a remarkable transformation. Her renewed spirit and determination mirrored my own journey of staying true to my purpose, even when faced with daunting obstacles.

This experience reinforced the importance of remaining focused on my mission. Through tailored mentorship, I help children and their families navigate their LIFE journey, encompassing personal and professional growth, spiritual enrichment, financial acumen, and health awareness. The ripple effect of this guidance is profound, empowering entire communities to thrive.

Military Leadership and Educational Foundation

My military background has been instrumental in shaping my leadership approach. The discipline, resilience, and strategic thinking I developed as a military leader have been invaluable in my mentorship work. In the military, I learned to lead with integrity, to remain steadfast in the face of adversity, and to inspire others to achieve their best. These principles have guided my efforts in mentoring over 5,000 children globally.

In addition to my military experience, my educational background in humanities, theology, and business law has enriched my mentorship approach. The study of humanities has given me deep insights into the human condition and the power of empathy. My theological education has provided a strong moral and ethical foundation, guiding me to lead with compassion and purpose. My knowledge of business law has equipped me with the skills to navigate complex organizational challenges and to advocate effectively for the children and families I serve.

Combining these diverse skills has allowed me to build a holistic mentorship program that addresses the multifaceted needs of at-risk children. Through this program, I have created a supportive community where children feel valued and empowered to pursue their dreams.

Mentoring Takeaways

Mentorship has taught me that true success comes from lifting others. One of the most profound lessons I've learned is encapsulated in the words of Dame Doria Cordova: "When you focus on being a blessing, God makes sure that you are always blessed in abundance." This philosophy drives my commitment to mentoring, ensuring that each interaction is an opportunity to sow seeds of hope and growth.

Another powerful quote from Dame Doria Cordova that resonates deeply with me is, "True wealth is having the ability to create, share, and transfer value to others." This belief underpins my efforts to instill financial literacy and entrepreneurial skills in the young minds I mentor, equipping them with tools to build a prosperous future.

One of my favorite biblical scriptures that guides my mentorship approach is Jeremiah 29:11: "For I know the plans I have for you," declares the Lord, "plans to prosper you and not to harm you, plans to give you hope and a future." This verse reminds me of the importance of instilling hope and a vision for the future in the children I mentor. It reassures them that despite their current circumstances, there is a greater plan for their lives filled with promise and potential.

Building Community

One of the most rewarding aspects of my mentorship work has been the creation of a supportive community for over 5,000 children. This community is built on the principles of mutual respect, collaboration, and shared growth. By fostering a sense of belonging and purpose, we have created an environment where children and their families can thrive.

Our community initiatives include educational workshops, health and wellness programs, financial literacy courses, and spiritual growth sessions. These programs are designed to address the holistic needs of the children and their families, providing them with the tools and resources they need to succeed.

One example of our community impact is the story of a young girl named Amanda. Amanda came from a troubled background and struggled with self-esteem and academic performance. Through our mentorship program, she received personalized support and guidance. We worked with her to develop a personalized education plan, provided tutoring services, and encouraged him to participate in our financial literacy workshops. Over time, Amanda's confidence grew, and her academic performance improved significantly. Today, Amanda is a thriving high school student with aspirations of becoming an engineer.

The journey of focusing on my purpose and working collaboratively with others has been instrumental in overcoming challenges and achieving success. By mentoring at-risk children globally and educating their families on crucial life skills, I've seen firsthand the transformative power of guided support and education. Staying true to my mission and leveraging the wisdom of mentors like Dame Doria Cordova has enabled me to create lasting impact and inspire future generations.

Through a combination of military leadership principles, educational insights, and a deep commitment to mentoring, I have built a thriving community that supports and empowers over 5,000 children. This work has been a labor of love, driven by the belief that every child deserves the opportunity to reach their full potential.

In conclusion, the journey of mentoring at-risk children has been one of the most fulfilling and transformative experiences of my life. By focusing on my purpose and harnessing the power of collaboration, I've been able to overcome numerous challenges and make a meaningful impact on the lives of thousands. My military leadership background, coupled with my educational achievements in humanities, theology, and business law, has provided me with the tools to build a vibrant community that nurtures and empowers young minds.

As leaders, we have the incredible opportunity to inspire and guide the next generation. It is through mentorship and the unwavering commitment to our purpose that we can create lasting change. Remember the words of Dame Doria Cordova: "When you focus on being a blessing, God makes sure that you are always blessed in abundance." Let this philosophy guide you as you strive to make a difference in your own communities.

To the readers who are inspired to take action, I encourage you to find your purpose, stay true to it, and use your unique skills and experiences to uplift others. By doing so, you not only enrich the lives of those you mentor but also create a ripple effect of positive change that extends far beyond your immediate reach. Embrace the journey and know that every step you take in service of others brings you closer to realizing the full potential of your leadership.

To the 13-year-old me, I would say: "Stay true to your dreams, even when the path is unclear. Your purpose will guide you through the toughest times, and the challenges you face today will become the foundation of your strength tomorrow. Believe in your ability to make a difference, and never stop learning."

Resources

1. *"The 7 Habits of Highly Effective People"* by Stephen R. Covey - This book provides timeless principles for personal and professional effectiveness that can enhance your leadership journey.

2. *"Dare to Lead"* by Brené Brown - Brené Brown's insights on courageous leadership and vulnerability are invaluable for anyone looking to make a meaningful impact.

3. *"The Purpose Driven Life"* by Rick Warren - This book offers a spiritual perspective on finding and living your purpose, which can be a powerful guide in your mentorship and leadership efforts.

Contact me: I would love to hear from you and support you on your leadership and mentorship journey. You can connect with me through the following platforms:
www.bettyspeaks.com
Instagram: @BettySpeaks
@alifechangenow

DR. BETTY SPEAKS

About Dr. Betty Speaks: Dr. Speaks is a United States Army retiree, the CEO of A Life Change Now, the Podcast Host of "Overcoming Battles by Being Strong and Courageous," The Artist and Songwriter of the single *"It's A Resurrection."* She is your Lifetime IMPRINT EMPRESS! She is very passionate about motivating individuals to resurrect and establish themselves spiritually, personally, or professionally. She's that chosen warrior who inspires others to create a life change now by leaving an INTENTIONAL IMPACTFUL IMPRINT for INFINITY. Betty is extremely passionate with helping individuals establish themselves and their generational wealth via multiple streams of income plus securing their retirement endeavors. She also mentors youthful ladies and other individuals or teams during transformational workshops, one-on-one mentorship, and other Total Well Being Events.

As an independent artist and songwriter, Dr. Betty Speaks is on a mission to share her transformational international leadership song, *"It's A Resurrection."* With a desire to reach a global audience, she uses her creative expression to inspire positive change worldwide. Dr. Speaks acknowledges the profound impact women have had on shaping the world for way over 200 years. Her song serves as an opportunity for her to provide testimony from a leader's perspective. She conveys the message that, despite life's most challenging endeavors, she can conquer and resurrect to lead because He's (God) alive in her. Dr. Betty Speaks invites listeners to embrace the powerful narrative, where the melody becomes a testament to her resilience and leadership. Through this song, she aims to spread the message of triumph over challenges and the ability to emerge stronger, echoing the resurrection theme in both life and leadership.

Author's Website: *www.BettySpeaks.com*
Book Series Website: *www.ThePrinciplesOfDebbieAndGoliath.com*

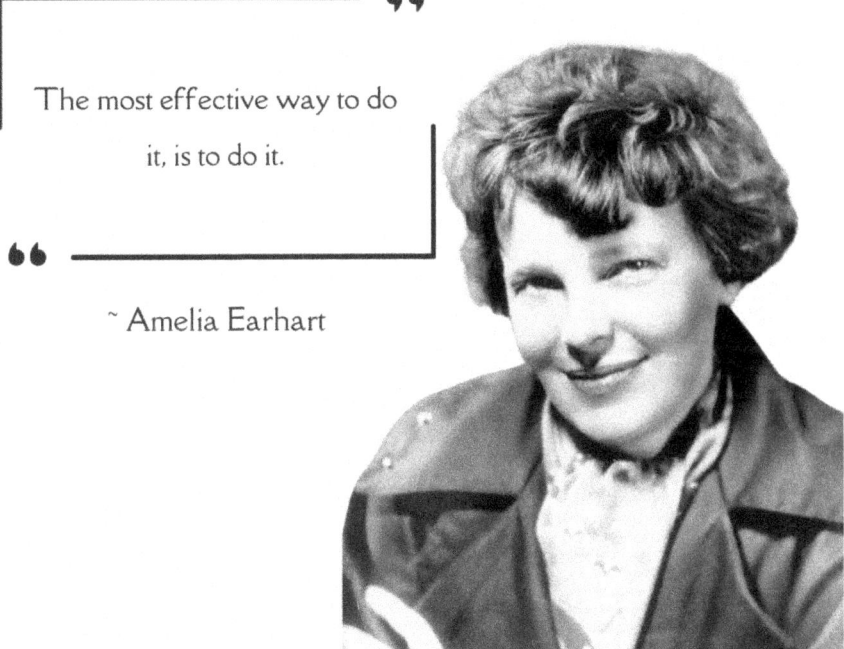

The most effective way to do it, is to do it.

~ Amelia Earhart

CHARLOTTE DELON

GETTING ALIGNED & CREATING FOCUS

When many think of focus and alignment, they often think of drawing alignment with others. It actually starts with you. Understanding your purpose, your why, will help to draw the alignment that is needed to get the job done. If you cannot lead yourself, you cannot lead others. If you cannot motivate yourself, you cannot motivate others.

When I was working to become a sales director at Mary Kay, I needed to get focused. First, I focused mentally, and then I focused on my actions. Mental, believe it or not, came first. I spent months trying to draw alignment with my family and friends on my decision to leave corporate and become a sales director and sell makeup.

At the time, I had a Master's in computer science and spent many years working in engineering and, now, I was going to "pedal lipstick," as my dad would call it. This lack of alignment was a blocker for me. I felt I needed my parents' approval to win! My mental focus at this time was weak as I sought the approval of others. Without focus, there was no alignment.

On this journey, I learned alignment first starts within. I could have continued to try to get my family to understand and remain stuck. I still remember the day that I took my father to an event where there were several Mary Kay millionaires. I thought, "He will have to see what I see to understand why I took the leap." It was very impressive. He was unphased by the excellence all around us. I had to accept that God didn't put the vision in him. He put it in me.

During that time, I was at an event, and the person speaking said, "Stop trying to sell the 20X20 dream to someone who lives their life on a 3X5 card." This statement forever changed my life. I quickly understood that it was not meant for those in my life to understand my journey. I caught the vision and needed to get into alignment and focus. Before this, it was almost a year of my trying to become a sales director. I would start in one area and quickly jump to another, never achieving success. Once I got into alignment with my vision and began to focus on my actions, I started seeing progress. The more progress I saw, the more confident I became.

As stated, before understanding and aligning my vision, I was all over the place. No focus. When you lack focus, you cannot identify where you have gaps. If you don't understand your gaps, you cannot improve. If you do not improve, you will not succeed. Continuous failure breeds frustration.

I got into alignment with my vision and dreams and began to focus. The focus was skills development. When I first became an engineer, I struggled a bit until I learned how to do my job. I thought, "How is this any different?" I must learn to be great at this opportunity, too.

My focus consisted of analyzing my own skill/opportunity gaps. I realized that because of the nature of my previous career, I didn't know a lot of women. I need to figure out how to meet women. I realized that, because of my insecurities around women, it was going to be awkward approaching them to offer my services. I received a lot of objections. The goal/my focus was how to overcome the objections. It became a game, after I got over myself, and I embraced having fun learning.

After I started learning about women, I learned how to market to them. I learned the art of customer service and how to apply makeup. Prior to Mary Kay, I didn't wear makeup. Considering that I'm teaching women of all nationalities how to apply makeup and skincare, I needed to be excellent so that they would trust me. I studied tutorials on makeup applications. I intentionally chose women who didn't look like me to learn new make-up application skills. I got really good at what I did.

Next, I learned how to deliver the message of why someone would want to join Mary Kay and be an independent sales consultant. I was growing my team and helping other leaders grow theirs. Within 3 months, I was in the top 2% and became a sales director. I also earned the use of a Mary Kay car. This was focus.

What one must get is, I could not do this without my team. I also could not achieve this without a vision to draw alignment and focus. If you can't see the path first, you cannot guide others.

Alignment and focus are reciprocal. You cannot have alignment if you are not focused on the goal at hand. Once you are aligned, focus is required to be intentional regarding each step you take to achieve the goal. Being intentional ensures that any action taken will align with a specific outcome. This requires learning how to say no to things that do not align with my target. I still assess today the value I'm getting out of an action or activity I'm partaking in—if it doesn't provide value, I move on.

This requires courage. If you do not have the courage to trust the process and your path, you will be all over the place following the guidance of many except yourself. This behavior does not drive alignment or focus.

I have come to the realization that there will be times when I will make a choice that makes absolutely no sense to anyone but me. As I stated earlier, God didn't put the vision in them. He put it in me. I've also learned that when I'm on a path that is out of alignment, I'm exhausted. Trust the cues your body is giving you. It will be your compass and, if you pay attention, you will get alignment and focus.

CHARLOTTE DELON

About Charlotte DeLon: Charlotte is a motivational speaker and coach with over 16 years of transformational leadership experience. She helps organizations transform culture for optimal output defining operational tenants and assessing behavioral gaps that can impede or accelerate change.

Charlotte is a Maxwell Leadership Certified Team Member and Certified Advance Behavioral Analysis DISC coach. Through the discovery of DISC results, Charlotte helps individuals define their superpowers and also what can be holding them back from being all that is possible.

Some key highlights:
Speaking: Keynote speaker, panel discussions for women in IT providing strategies on how to manage work, family and life, launched leader to leader series discussing Leadership Philosophy's and benefits.

Coaching: Executive leadership coaching to improve organizational health. Career and life coach helping people succeed in career and managing life challenges like fear.

Teaching: Facilitate Leadership Acumen Mastermind series Train on leadership styles (situational, transformational and servant). Teach how to build Leadership Philosophy's to deliver and drive inner and outer accountability.

Favorite quote: "No one cares how much you know until they know how much you care." ~ Theodore Roosevelt.

Author's Website: *www.LeadershipByCharlotteDelon.com*

Book Series Website: *www.ThePrinciplesOfDebbieAndGoliath.com*

CYNTHIA GALLARDO

THE POWER OF FOCUS & ALIGNMENT AS A LEGACYPRENEUR

Every one of us faces Goliaths—challenges that loom large, casting shadows over our dreams and ambitions. As a younger version of myself, these giants seemed invincible, their presence a constant test of will and perseverance. Yet, it was through focus and alignment, coupled with the power of synergy, that I discovered not just the path to overcoming these obstacles but also the blueprint for building a lasting legacy.

Every Goliath in my journey—be it self-doubt, societal pressures, or tangible obstacles—taught me the invaluable lesson of resilience. These giants didn't tower over me to signal my defeat but to challenge my resolve and to sharpen my strategy. From the personal battles of overcoming fear and insecurity to professional challenges of carving a niche in a world that often seemed unwelcoming, each Goliath was a lesson in disguise.

Our lives are a tapestry of challenges and victories, each thread woven with the lessons learned and the battles fought. As I pen this chapter across the expanse of time, I bring forth not just my victories but the essence of every hurdle I've overcome, hoping to light your path and arm you with the wisdom of hindsight.

The Essence of Focus and Alignment

My journey's first lesson was understanding the power of focus. Focus is not just about dedication to a task but about aligning every effort, every thought, and every action towards a singular goal. It's about saying no to the myriad distractions that life throws your way and saying yes to what truly matters.

Alignment and focus are two pivotal concepts, especially in the context of personal and professional development, project management, and organizational strategy. Understanding each and exploring how they interrelate can provide a blueprint for achieving goals more efficiently and effectively.

Alignment refers to the process of ensuring that all elements of an organization, project, or personal endeavor are arranged in a way that supports the achievement of goals and objectives. It's about creating coherence among strategies, processes, and actions. In an organizational context, alignment involves ensuring that the company's mission, vision, values, and strategies are all in sync and that resources are allocated in a way that supports the overall direction. For individuals, alignment means ensuring that one's actions, efforts, and resources are directed towards their goals and values.

Focus, on the other hand, is the concentration of attention or energy on something or someone. It is the ability to direct thought and effort towards specific objectives, tasks, or activities without getting distracted by less relevant or non-essential issues. Focus is what enables an individual or organization to maintain a clear vision of what they want to achieve and to dedicate the necessary resources and energy towards achieving it.

Alignment and focus are deeply interconnected and mutually reinforcing. Alignment sets the framework or direction for efforts and decisions, ensuring that actions are coherent and synergistically aimed at a common goal. Focus, then, is the mechanism through which the energy and efforts are channeled within that framework to achieve those goals.

When a person aligns their actions and efforts with their personal values and goals, focus becomes much more effective. This alignment ensures that the focus is not scattered or wasted on irrelevant pursuits. Instead, the focused effort is directed towards activities that are meaningful and aligned with personal aspirations, leading to greater fulfillment and success.

In a business context, alignment ensures that all departments and team members are working towards the same strategic objectives. When the organization's efforts are aligned, focus can then be applied to prioritize projects, tasks, and initiatives that directly contribute to the achievement of those objectives. This prevents resources from being wasted on misaligned activities and enables the organization to move more cohesively towards its goals.

The synergy between alignment and focus is essential for any successful endeavor. Alignment provides the roadmap, while focus drives the journey. Together, they ensure that efforts are not just efficient but also effective, leading to the achievement of desired outcomes with greater precision and satisfaction.

Resources that were instrumental in concentrating on alignment and focus included time management, mindfulness practices to enhance concentration, and setting SMART goals to clarify my ambitions. Books like *The Seven Habits of Highly Effective People* by Stephen Covey and *The Coffee Bean: A Simple Lesson to Create a Positive Change* by Jon Gordon provided blueprints for cultivating a focused mindset.

Synergy: The Collective Force

No battle against a Goliath is fought alone. The synergy created through collaboration has been my fortress and my strength. This realization came not just from victories but from the shared struggles and combined efforts of those around me—mentors, peers, and communities who believed in a common goal.

Engaging in women-focused networking groups and finding mentors through platforms like LinkedIn and Mentorship programs offered by professional associations became cornerstones of my support system. These connections were not merely for guidance but for creating a feedback loop that helped refine my focus and align my efforts with my ultimate goals.

Incorporating the Legacypreneur™ Blueprint

The cornerstone of every victory was not solitary struggle but the power of synergy—working together with mentors, peers, and communities. I learned early on that the weight of the world becomes lighter when shared with others. The journey of overcoming obstacles and building a legacy is beautifully encapsulated in the Legacypreneur™ Blueprint, which integrates the principles of SY-NE-R-G-Y™.

1. Save Yourself (SY): Self-care and personal growth were my starting points. Investing in personal development through lifelong learning and attending workshops and seminars on leadership and self-improvement laid the groundwork for my journey. But the greatest resource was the mentorship from those who had walked this path before me. They taught me the importance of self-care and setting a strong foundation upon which I could support others.

2. Next Everyone Else (NE): Empowering others became a mission parallel to my personal growth. Initiatives like mentoring young women in my field, engaging in community service, and leading by example in promoting equality in the workplace underscored the importance of lifting as I climbed. The realization dawned that my battles were not mine alone. By reaching out and supporting others, I was building a community. This was not just about networking but about creating a support system where success was shared. Programs like mentorship initiatives and community support groups were invaluable, offering both a platform to give and receive guidance.

3. Reassess/Reevaluate/Repeat (R): The iterative process of assessment and adaptation kept my goals in focus and my actions aligned. Tools like reflective journaling, performance tracking apps, and regular strategy sessions with my team or mentors ensured continuous improvement. Each challenge conquered was a lesson learned, and

each setback was an opportunity to reassess and adapt. Continuous learning through online courses, webinars, and even feedback from my community kept me agile and resilient. This iterative process of learning and growing became a staple of my strategy against every Goliath.

4. Give (G): Generosity in sharing knowledge, resources, and time with others not only enriched my journey but also amplified my impact. Participating in and contributing to forums like Lean In circles and other female empowerment networks underscored the value of giving back. The essence of my journey was encapsulated in giving back. Whether it was through volunteering, mentorship, or simply sharing my knowledge and resources, I found empowerment in empowerment.

5. Yes/Yes/Yes (Celebrate) (Y): Celebrating every milestone, no matter how small, cultivated a culture of positivity and gratitude. This step reinforced the importance of acknowledging progress and maintaining morale, both personally and within my community. This step was about reinforcing the positive impact of our collective efforts and inspiring continued action towards our goals.

Empowerment Resources for Females

To empower other females on their journeys, I leaned on and recommend the following resources that promote lifelong learning:

• Educational Platforms: Coursera, edX, Udemy, Khan Academy, and Stanford Online for expanding knowledge and skills.

• Professional Networks: Joining industry-specific associations and groups like the American Bar Association for law, BNI (Business Network International), or the National Entrepreneurs Association (NEA) offer mentorship and networking opportunities.

• Empowerment Programs: Engaging with organizations like Women and Girls Empowered (WAGE) offered by the American Bar

Association or Girls on the Run, which provide support and resources for young women aspiring to make a difference.

- Mentorship Programs: Both formal and informal, these were crucial in providing guidance, support, and valuable insights.

The Legacy of Our Battles

Looking back, the giants I faced were not just obstacles but opportunities —each challenge a steppingstone towards building a legacy rooted in strength, resilience, and collective success. Through focus, alignment, and the power of synergy, I've learned that the greatest legacy we can leave is not just in the successes we achieve, but in the empowerment and upliftment of those who walk the path with us and after us.

To my younger self and to every teen girl facing her Goliaths: Know that with focus, alignment, and the support of those around you, no giant is too mighty. Let the Legacypreneur™ Blueprint guide you, let your journey be enriched by the wisdom of others, and let your legacy be defined by the lives you've touched and the difference you've made.

CYNTHIA GALLARDO

About Cynthia Gallardo: Cynthia Gallardo, your Leading Legacy Lawyer™, is keynote speaker, author, business strategist, legacypreneur™, and lawyer. Cynthia is passionate about providing a positive interaction with every person she meets on a daily basis, whether in a personal, professional, or academic setting. Cynthia's creed is "Results. Not excuses." Cynthia is a catalyst that empowers and inspires entrepreneurs struggling to transform a business idea to a vision to a reality to a profitable business by discovering their unique business DNA to launch, build, and protect their legacy. Cynthia graduated with honors earning her MBA and law degree. Cynthia is a proud graduate of Southern University Law Center. Cynthia is CEO and founder of Cynthia Gallardo Law, LLC and Synergy Solutions PRO, LLC which houses Launch to Legacy Academy™. Cynthia practices immigration law, transactional law, and estate planning. Cynthia takes a holistic approach to business and shares her 5 Step Launch to Legacy™ Blueprint outlining the framework to live and leave a lasting legacy. Cynthia worked in the corporate environment for nearly fifteen years transitioning from front-line representative to management roles to a leadership role. Cynthia is a lifelong learner and strives to guide others to become the best versions of themselves personally and professionally.

Cynthia lives in Louisiana with her husband and son where they enjoy spending time together in spiritual activities. In addition, the Gallardo family has four furbabies–three Doberman pinschers and a cat. The Gallardo family is a strong advocate of the foster-to-adoption program as they have personally taken the foster-to-adoption journey.

Author's Website: *www.CynthiaGallardo.com*

Book Series Website: *www.ThePrinciplesOfDebbieAndGoliath.com*

DEBORAH J. ANDERSON

ALIGNMENT THROUGH THE POWER OF PRAYER

Focus and alignment have been essential principles in my journey of overcoming personal and professional challenges. As a coach, speaker, author, and motivator, I have learned the immense value of collaboration, prioritization, and faith.

These principles have guided me in navigating various obstacles and achieving my goals. Through collaboration, I have been able to leverage the strengths of others and create impactful projects that benefit both myself and those around me. Prioritization has allowed me to focus on what truly matters, ensuring that my time and energy are invested in activities that align with my values and aspirations. Lastly, faith has been my beacon of light during the darkest moments, providing me with the strength and resilience to persevere in the face of adversity. By embracing these principles wholeheartedly, I have transformed challenges into opportunities for growth and success.

Finding Focus Through Collaboration

One of the key themes I emphasize is the power of collaboration in solving problems. In my role as a special education administrator, I frequently facilitated meetings involving diverse teams tasked with making significant decisions for students. These teams included regular classroom teachers, special education teachers, speech pathologists, physical therapists, occupational therapists, school psychologists, administrators, social workers, and parents.

I recall a time when I would enter these meetings with my own agenda, believing I knew the best decisions for the child we'd be counseling and discussing. However, I soon realized that approaching the situation with an open mind and listening to the team's input resulted in better outcomes. Over time, I found that coming in with my own agenda in these meetings must be revised.

So, I had the experience of conversing about our agendas with the team. I suggested that each of us take ownership of our respective areas of expertise. By approaching our teamwork objectively, we each presented our information without personal biases on what should be done or any preconceived decisions. Our focus on being present and attentive, ensuring that the whole team hears and values our information, was a winning score.

This approach led to collaborative decision-making, where each team member's perspective contributed to a more comprehensive and effective solution. I believe this problem-solving method extends beyond professional settings into personal decisions as well. By surrounding myself with wise, faith-based individuals, I ensure that my decisions are well-rounded and thoughtful.

Prioritization: A Key to Alignment

In addition to collaboration, I underscore the importance of prioritization in achieving alignment. My approach to planning and organizing has evolved over the years. I used to do it independently and methodically, and even in my twenties, I would plan things out in advance. And I don't do that anymore. I'm much more spontaneous now. I'll have a general game plan.

This shift in mindset was influenced by my faith, which taught me to trust in God's plan rather than rigidly sticking to my own. The saying resonates with me: "You plan, and God laughs." Recognizing that God already has a plan, I focus on being open to divine guidance and allowing my plans to align with a higher purpose.

One practical example involves a project called Digital Church, which required me to close the door on a previous commitment to make room for this new opportunity. Despite knowing I could manage both, I chose to prioritize the project that brought me more joy and fulfillment. Could I have fit both projects easily into my calendar? Absolutely, yes! But I also wasn't finding joy in the other. I went ahead and did the thing that I knew I wanted to close the door on just because I was a responsible leader, and well, I committed to doing it.

This decision-making process, guided by prioritization and alignment with my values, allows me to focus on what truly matters and pursue opportunities that elevate me personally and professionally.

This intentional decision-making process, guided by prioritization and alignment with my values, has truly been transformative. I have unlocked new personal and professional growth levels by prioritizing joy and fulfillment over mere obligation. Embracing opportunities that resonate with my core values has brought me a sense of purpose and allowed me to thrive in my personal and professional pursuits. Closing the door on commitments that no longer serve me has been a liberating experience, freeing up time and energy to invest in endeavors that bring me genuine happiness and fulfillment. This journey of intentional decision-making continues to shape my path, guiding me toward opportunities that align with my true passions and aspirations.

Embracing Faith in Problem-Solving

My faith plays a central role in my approach to overcoming challenges. Prayer is my first response when faced with difficulties. That's the very first thing that I do. This reliance on prayer gives me the clarity and strength to tackle problems head-on.

When I pray, I feel a sense of peace wash over me, like a reassuring hug from the universe. In these moments of stillness and connection, I find the courage to confront my challenges with a clear mind and a steadfast heart. Prayer is not just a ritual for me; it's a source of comfort and guidance, a beacon of hope in times of uncertainty. With each whispered prayer, I draw strength from deep within, knowing I am never alone in my struggles. And so, armed with faith and fortified by prayer, I face each obstacle with unwavering resolve, ready to overcome whatever stands in my way.

I also emphasize the importance of discerning from whom to seek advice, ensuring that the people I turn to are faith-based and trustworthy. For me, are they faith-based? Are they trustworthy? Now, those people will have to be faith-based, and they will have to be in alignment with me.

When seeking advice, it's crucial to surround yourself with individuals who share your values and beliefs and possess wisdom and insight that can guide you in the right direction. Choosing faith-based and trustworthy individuals to seek advice from can provide you with perspectives that align with your principles and help you make decisions that resonate with your beliefs. It's essential to have a circle of individuals who support you and challenge you to grow and learn. You can navigate life's challenges with confidence and clarity by seeking counsel from those grounded in faith and possessing greater wisdom. So, remember to surround yourself with people who uplift and inspire you, guiding you toward a path of growth and fulfillment.

My faith guides my decisions and influences how I handle setbacks. Instead of complaining about challenges, I seek support from my spiritual community, asking for their prayers and focusing on positive outcomes. In terms of my spirituality and support, they know me better than anybody, so instead of complaining, I do share with them what unfolds. I highly recommend you refine your prayers and be aware and attentive to whom you seek advice.

> *"But seek ye first the kingdom of God, and his righteousness; and all these things shall be added unto you."*
> ~ Matthew 6:33

Overcoming Personal Goliaths

Throughout my life, I have faced numerous personal Goliaths, from professional challenges to personal struggles. My ability to overcome these obstacles is rooted in my faith, focus, and alignment with my core values. One powerful story from my time in special education administration highlights the value of collaboration and its impact on making critical decisions for students. This experience taught me the invaluable lesson that true strength lies in unity and collaboration.

As we navigate life's challenges, may we always remember the power of coming together, leveraging our collective strengths, and embracing diverse perspectives to overcome our personal Goliaths with grace and resilience.

I also reflect on my journey of personal growth, transitioning from being called Debbie to Deb and finally embracing my true identity as Deborah. This transformation represents my evolution from a time of difficulty and uncertainty to a place of empowerment and self-awareness. I grew up being called Debbie. Then, people started to refer to me as Deb. Being called "Deb" came during a challenging time of my life when I was not happy.

Now, as I proudly introduce myself as Deborah, my God-given name, I am fully embracing my authenticity and stepping into my own power. The name Deborah holds a sense of strength, wisdom, and resilience that truly resonates with who I have become. This evolution symbolizes my journey of overcoming challenges, learning to love and accept myself, and finding inner peace. By embracing my true identity as Deborah, I am honoring my growth and celebrating the woman I have become.

My story is a testament to the power of resilience and the importance of believing in oneself. By aligning my actions with my faith and values, I have navigated life's challenges and emerged stronger. Through every trial and tribulation, I held onto the belief that I had the strength and determination to overcome any obstacle in my path with God's help. With unwavering conviction in my abilities, I faced each adversity head-on, refusing to be defined by circumstances beyond my control.

As I walked the path of resilience, I discovered a well of inner strength that I never knew existed within me. It was this resilience that carried me through the darkest of times, shining a light of hope even in the bleakest moments. With each setback, I found an opportunity for growth, a chance to learn more about myself and the world around me.

Through it all, I learned that true resilience is about bouncing back from adversity and using those experiences to build a stronger, more resilient self. It is about embracing challenges as opportunities for growth and transformation, knowing that each hurdle we overcome only serves to make us more resilient in the face of future obstacles.

As I look back on my journey, I am filled with gratitude for the challenges that have shaped me into the resilient individual I am today. I carry with me the lessons learned, and the strength gained, knowing that no matter what life may throw my way, I have the resilience and belief in myself and the power of God to overcome any obstacle that comes my way.

My insights and experiences provide valuable lessons in conquering your challenges. Here are some practical steps to help you apply these principles in your life:

1. **Embrace Collaboration:** Seek input from diverse perspectives and collaborate with others to find comprehensive solutions to problems. Surround yourself with wise, faith-based individuals who can provide valuable insights.

2. **Prioritize Effectively:** Identify the most important tasks and focus on those that align with your values and bring you joy. Be willing to close doors on commitments that no longer serve your higher purpose.

3. **Rely on Faith:** Incorporate prayer and spiritual guidance into your decision-making process. Trust that God has a plan for you, and be open to divine guidance.

4. **Believe in Yourself:** Recognize your own strength and resilience. Embrace your true identity and believe in your ability to overcome challenges.

5. **Seek Support:** Lean on your spiritual community and trusted individuals for support and encouragement. Share your struggles and ask for prayers and positive energy to help you navigate difficult times.

My journey of focus and alignment offers a powerful example of how collaboration, prioritization, and faith can help overcome personal and professional challenges. By embracing these principles, you can find the strength and clarity to tackle your own obstacles and achieve your goals. Remember, the power to overcome lies within you, and with the proper focus and alignment, you can conquer any Goliath that comes your way.

DR. DEBORAH J. ANDERSON

About Dr. Deborah J. Anderson: Dr. Deborah J. Anderson has worked as a special education teacher, administrator, and university professor. As a professional speaker, life coach, and author, Deborah inspires others to achieve a higher level of success through maximum productivity, action, and capitalizing on one's strengths. Deborah resides in her home state of Nebraska, where she has used her retirement as an opportunity to "refire:" serving others through various ministries.

In addition, she leads and facilitates Fresh Start groups for women who are experiencing the effects of offense, hurt, and loss through the transforming power of Jesus. Deborah is going ALL IN and saying "Yes" to whatever God is calling her to do. Deborah is dedicating this chapter to her granddaughter, Jancye.

Author's Website: *www.LinkedIn.com/in/Dr-Deborah-J-Anderson*

Book Series Website: *www.ThePrinciplesOfDebbieAndGoliath.com*

EILEEN E. GALBRAITH

CLEARING THE PATH: HOW FOCUS SHAPES OUR JOURNEY

Maintaining focus isn't always a straightforward task. My journey of personal transformation spans over 24 years, ignited by pivotal moments like divorce and financial hardships leading to bankruptcy. Amidst the chaos, my relentless curiosity and commitment to seeking answers propelled me forward.

Had I clung to old mindsets of defeat and isolation, or worse, succumbed to despair, including my own battle with attempting to take my life in 1998, my story might have ended prematurely.

During that period of my life, my attention was consumed by questioning why this situation was unfolding, compounded by the shock and myriad emotions accompanying the revelation of my husband's desire for a divorce. Despite my lack of understanding regarding the root cause, my focus remained steadfast in rectifying everything.

My sole focus was fixated on this situation, causing detrimental effects elsewhere in my life. My work and health deteriorated significantly—I plummeted to 100lbs, underwent gallbladder removal, and developed anemia all within a years' time. These were all consequences of my unwavering attention solely on this matter, neglecting everything else.

Change was imperative, and I held the sole power to initiate it.

After this trauma passed, I chose a path of personal development, immersing myself in the guidance of mentors and leaders who illuminated the way. Through introspection, I realized the power in reshaping my thoughts, beliefs, and inner dialogue—shedding the weight of negativity that hindered progress.

On this transformative journey, I discovered the profound impact of community and support. I learned to reach out and ask for help, understanding that facing trauma alone was unnecessary.
Shifting my focus, I recognized that the true obstacle wasn't the world around me but rather my own perspectives. Aligning with my authentic purpose became my compass.

In embracing our capacity for growth, we come to realize that each of us holds within ourselves the potential to transcend our current limitations and situations. It begins by directing our attention towards those aspects of life that ignite a profound sense of joy and fulfillment within us. By nurturing these passions and aligning our actions with them, we unlock a gateway to a multitude of unforeseen opportunities.

As we wholeheartedly immerse ourselves in activities and pursuits that resonate deeply with our true selves, we invite a harmonious alignment with the universe. This alignment acts as a catalyst, propelling us toward pathways previously unimagined. Doors once thought closed suddenly swing open, revealing pathways to personal and professional fulfillment that had remained hidden in the shadows of doubt and uncertainty.

The journey towards self-actualization is not merely about achieving predefined goals or conforming to societal expectations. It's about tapping into the boundless reservoir of potential that resides within us and allowing our passions to guide us towards our true purpose. In doing so, we not only expand our own horizons but also inspire those around us to embark on their own transformative journeys.

So, let us embrace the power of focus and alignment, recognizing that by cultivating joy and purpose in our lives, we pave the way for a future brimming with limitless possibilities.

Embracing new opportunities became a mantra, inviting remarkable individuals and experiences into my life. I now find myself enveloped by a network of support, steadfast through life's storms. We all possess the potential to transcend our current selves by directing our focus towards sources of genuine joy. Aligning with these passions can unveil unforeseen opportunities, transforming our reality.

I am deeply grateful for the privilege to now support others on their journeys. There's profound fulfillment in knowing that by embodying my true self, I can uplift and guide others toward their own discovery.

Let us continue our journey of self-discovery unceasingly, for within it lies the road to fulfillment and purpose. By prioritizing what brings us joy, we become catalysts for profound service to others. Embrace this truth, as it stands to be your invaluable gift to humanity.

At times, we stray from the true focal point of our lives, allowing external forces to steer our decisions. Our surroundings, societal pressures, media, and the opinions of those close to us all exert influence. Yet, there comes a juncture where we must reconnect with our inner intuition, crafting our own beliefs, values, and mindset. It's crucial to prioritize what holds utmost significance for us, rather than conforming to external expectations.

During this challenging period, I discovered several important aspects about myself:

1. I possess the power to enact the changes I desire.

2. Others' perceptions of me, whether positive or negative, are their responsibility, not mine.

3. I've honed the ability to detach from emotions in a situation, enabling me to think rationally and assess it objectively.

4. I've gained insight into my boundaries and how I allow others to treat me.

5. I prioritize open communication and believe that everyone deserves to have their voice heard.

6. I've developed a deep appreciation for myself, embracing my unique qualities and contributions to humanity. I genuinely believe in my worth and value.

I consistently advise my clients to extend themselves some grace. Regardless of past experiences or present challenges, it's essential to prioritize honoring oneself.

Every journey begins with a starting point. Below, I've outlined several steps to help you enhance your focus; as I understand, you may be wondering, "How exactly do I achieve this?"

Here are a few tips:

1. Set Clear Goals: Define specific, achievable goals that align with your priorities and values. Having a clear direction will help you stay focused on what truly matters to you.

Setting clear goals is crucial for maintaining focus and achieving success in any endeavor. When you define specific, achievable goals that align with your priorities and values, you provide yourself with a roadmap for action.

Clear goals provide you with a sense of direction and purpose. They help you understand what you want to accomplish and why it's important to you. Without clear goals, you may feel lost or uncertain about your path forward.

When your goals align with your priorities and values, you experience a greater sense of fulfillment and satisfaction upon achieving them. Aligning your goals with what truly matters to you ensures that your efforts are meaningful and purposeful.

2. Prioritize Tasks: Identify the most important tasks and tackle them first. Prioritizing your responsibilities will prevent you from feeling overwhelmed and help you concentrate on what needs to be done.

Prioritizing tasks is crucial for effective time management and productivity. By identifying the most important and urgent tasks, individuals can allocate their time and resources efficiently, ensuring that critical objectives are addressed promptly.

Prioritization helps prevent feeling overwhelmed by a long list of responsibilities, allowing individuals to focus on what truly matters. It enables better decision-making, as individuals can allocate their energy towards tasks that align with their goals and values. Ultimately, prioritizing tasks enhances productivity, reduces stress, and increases the likelihood of achieving desired outcomes in both personal and professional endeavors.

3. Minimize Distractions: Create a conducive environment for focus by minimizing distractions. This could involve turning off notifications, setting specific times for checking emails and social media, or finding a quiet space to work.

4. Practice Mindfulness: Cultivate mindfulness through techniques such as meditation, deep breathing, or mindful awareness. Being present in the moment can enhance your ability to concentrate and stay focused on the task at hand.

5. Break Tasks into Manageable Steps: Break down larger tasks into smaller, more manageable steps. This makes it easier to stay focused and maintain momentum as you work towards your goals.

6. Take Regular Breaks: Allow yourself to take regular breaks to recharge and refresh your mind. Short breaks can help prevent burnout and maintain productivity levels throughout the day.

7. Stay Organized: Keep your workspace and schedule organized to minimize clutter and chaos. Having a structured environment can promote focus and streamline your workflow.

By implementing these tips into your daily routine, you can cultivate greater focus and achieve your goals more effectively. I go into these and several more in my G.A.P. Program—reach out, I would love to support you.

I trust you've discovered value in this discourse. "What we put our attention to grows stronger in our lives," as quoted by my mentor, Janet Bray Attwood. Consider: Where do you channel your focus, and what manifests in your life as a result?

EILEEN E. GALBRAITH

About Eileen E Galbraith: As a Financial Architect for Business, entrepreneurs hire Eileen to build their influence and scale their profits because most lack essential methods and channels to create success, lack funding opportunities, and may face continuous struggles resulting in business disarray. So, Eileen helps them define, align, and design a visible, credible, and sustaining business. Financial disarray is a precursor to failure—do not let that happen to your business!

Eileen is a Compassionate Kick-ass Coach. She can kick your butt in financial shape and make things happen, but she's also very compassionate. She knows what people need, what they want, and how to deliver it.

Eileen is a Certified FICO Pro, an International Best-Selling Author and Speaker, a sought-after Business Success Coach, and the Founder of Renewed Abundance and Credit Knowhow. She has run multi-million-dollar businesses throughout her career and increased cash flow and profitability throughout her markets. Recognized as a professional Business Coach, Eileen positions her clients toward optimal possibilities, such as optimizing their personal credit to position themselves to build credit in the name of their business. This all-important step opens the doors to Financial Creditability, Fundability, and Business Growth. Eileen has a high-energy, no-nonsense approach and loves supporting people with their goals. Just look for the Dancing Queen, and you will find Eileen!

Author's Website: *www.CreditKnowHow.biz &*
www.RenewedAbundance.com

Book Series Website: *www.ThePrinciplesOfDebbieAndGoliath.com*

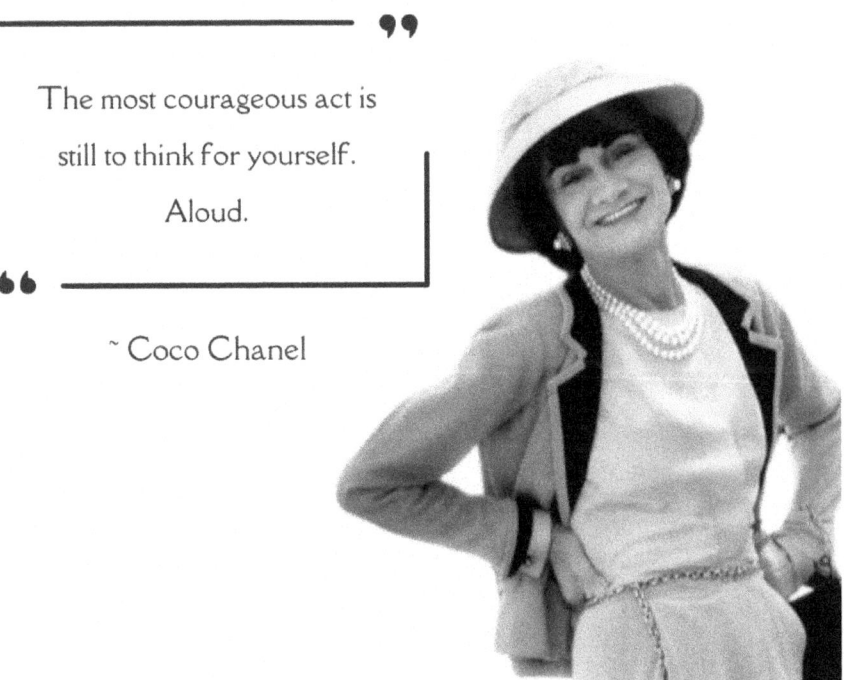

The most courageous act is
still to think for yourself.
Aloud.

~ Coco Chanel

ELIZABETH ANNE WALKER

THE POWER OF READING & PERSONAL DEVELOPMENT

There is a modern movement called baby-led growth. This is where the parents of a young child allow the child to develop at their own pace with minimal intervention until the child is ready. For example, not sitting the child up until the child does it themselves, not propping the child into the crawling position, and not reading to a child until they express an interest in books. This is indeed an interesting movement and is vastly different from what both I received as a child and the way I parented my own children.

Reading was very important in my family, and I recall being read to at a very young age. I, myself, as a parent read to my children from the day they were born. In their little hospital cots, we did reading time. Why? Because the vast knowledge and believe it or not worldly experience I had gained from being read to and reading books was so valuable to me I wanted to impress that upon my children. I wanted their brains to grow and develop in the way mine had. I wanted them to have the best opportunities in life and to me that all started with the ability to read.

As a child, we had a family book that came out every Christmas. It was called *Santa's Workshop*. I still have it and I am excited to read it to my grandchild who is due in a few months. This book smelled old, it had a few color plate illustrations and large writing so as a child I could read along. As the eldest grandchild, years later I would read it to my nephews and niece. The joy and wonder in this one book led to a love and curiosity of just what might be on the pages of every other book I have ever read.

The development of a person is vast and convoluted and is steeped in tradition both societal and familial. And it is not until we are of an adult nature, let's say somewhere between 15 and 20 that we realize the value of our own development. The problem is at this point our challenges may have already been created and may be as big as Goliath in nature. So, we start down the personal development route and "try" to learn as much as we can. It often starts with books and if you've never read before (accepting what you were forced to read in school) then here is challenge number one!

No need to worry, you can get an audiobook. Have you ever wondered what the difference between an audiobook and reading is? It's the development of the characters and scene using your own voice in your head, your own memories, and your own ideas that is the difference. When you listen to an audiobook with someone else's voice you tend to create imagery in your mind that you assume someone with that voice would create, as opposed to that which you would naturally create. Rather than a major problem, it's just a minor limitation.

And it's ok you will gain some value as your brain continues to personally develop. Or will you? You see if the love of books is not created as a child, statistics say you are less likely to enjoy any kind of reading whether it is traditional or audio. And the irony of this is I am here writing this information in a book!

So, where are we at? You can avoid your Goliath if you learn to read? If your mum or dad valued reading you will too? That if you read you automatically personally develop. That's what I thought too!

There is another pathway to personal development though, one that we often pretend does not exist and one that we rarely celebrate. It is the path of ongoing Goliaths. The path of continuous hard knocks and challenges, the path of adversity. The path my son took. He hated reading, he refused to read, and I doubt now that he is 23 that he has ever read a book since he was 5 or 6 years old. Personal development though is far from foreign to him, it wasn't always this way.

14 years old living in Sydney Australia, living with mum half the time and dad half the time, angry at the world because his parents couldn't love him enough to stay together. Gets into the wrong crowd and starts using drugs. Mum from an upper-middle-class old-fashioned values family has no idea what to do except blame herself for being a terrible mum. Dad from a working-class family joins in. While I destroy myself with guilt ("maybe I should have accepted the abuse to keep the family together") my son destroys himself with substances.

Well, I read and read and read and read. Everything I could find on parenting, teenage drug use, etc., etc., and nothing made sense or helped me to feel any better. He partied, and partied, and partied, and partied, and nothing he did made him feel any better. My hair fell out and I became incredibly unwell. He lost weight dramatically and became incredibly unwell. There was nothing I could do for him, by now he barely answered a text let alone a call and he hadn't slept a night at home in about a year.

I had to do the one thing the books said that I hadn't done, I had to start living for me. Personal development became an integral part of my life, I did the courses, I read the books, I went to seminars and trainings, and little by little as I got better and learned to love myself more, so did he! The more I invested in me the more I was able to help him without actually even speaking to him.

Fast forward to now. I run one of the biggest personal development businesses in Australia, my son works for me as our Nurture manager and spends most of his time helping mammas who have lost their sons to drugs or other distractions. Every single time, as the momma evolves so does the son.

I am so grateful for the gift of reading I had, my gateway to personal development. I am so grateful for the experiences my son had, and his gateway to personal development. I am so grateful that we work together to make a large impact on the world and help others find their gateways to a happy and fulfilling life.

P.S. He got married a little while ago and now we are expecting his son and my first grand-baby in March 2024.

ELIZABETH ANNE WALKER

About Elizabeth Anne Walker: Elizabeth is Australia's leading Female Integrated NLP Trainer, an international speaker with Real Success, and the host of Success Resources's (Australia's largest and most successful events promoter, including speakers such as Tony Robbins and Sir Richard Branson) inaugural Australian Women's Program "The Seed." Elizabeth has guided many people to achieve complete personal breakthroughs and phenomenal personal and business growth. With over 25 years of experience transforming the lives of hundreds of thousands of people, Elizabeth's goal is to assist leaders to create the reality they choose to live, impacting millions on a global scale.

A thought leader who has worked alongside people like Gary Vaynerchuck, Kerwin Rae, Jeffery Slayter, and Kate Gray, Elizabeth has an outstanding method of delivering heart with business.

As a former lecturer in medicine at the University of Sydney and lecturer in nursing at Western Sydney University, Elizabeth was instrumental in the research and development of the stillbirth and neonatal death pathways, ensuring each family in Australia went home knowing what happened to their child, and felt understood, heard, and seen.

A former Australian Champion in Trampolining and Australian Dance sport, Elizabeth has always been passionate about the mindset and skills required to create the results you are seeking.

Author's Website: *www.ElizabethAnneWalker.com*

Book Series Website: *www.ThePrinciplesOfDebbieAndGoliath.com*

FATIMA HURD

INTEGRITY SELLS

Sometimes, we spend a great part of lives wondering, "What am I good at?" But it's my humble opinion that we already know that at an early age, especially when you realize all through your life there have been signs guiding you along the way.

But when you are not in alignment, you can very easily "choose" to overlook those signs. That is what happened to me. It started when I was in grade school, and I remember it was a week before school was out for the summer. A couple of weeks prior, we completed our state testing. We were also given another test similar to the disc program as a bonus—it didn't count against our grade, as it highlighted personality traits. Based on that result, it suggested the professions that you would be great at.

I recall sitting there, waiting to get my results, as I watched others who got their results first get excited as they were given options to be teachers, doctors, and a variety of other great professions. I thought for sure I'd get maybe an author or something in that realm since I loved to read and write. When I got my results, it highlighted my traits and it indicated that I'd be great in anything that was sales related or as a vendor. I was shocked—at this young age, I didn't understand the word vendor that well; sales, yes: "you sell something," but what does that mean?

No one in my family that I knew of was in sales. Both my parents worked in factories and worked hard. The only thing that came to mind was the vending machine guy who would come in and fill up the school vending machines. I remember being devastated. Now, don't take me wrong—I respect that guy and the fact that he earned his living honestly, but while my classmates were getting results that was putting them on a trajectory to be lawyers and doctors, I was going to be a vending machine employee!

My heart was crushed. I threw the paper away and went home that day feeling sad. That's where I feel the disconnect was with my alignment in sales. When I became an adult, I was always being prospected and encouraged to go into every job you can think of that was in sales. Of course, over the years my experience and negative perception of salespeople didn't improve. I always felt that they would tell you anything to sell you whatever they wanted to sell you. That was my opinion; I didn't trust them, so why would people trust me?

My feeling, thoughts, and opinions about sales just weren't aligned with my values. I remember at 18 being asked to take my real estate license by a broker who saw the potential in me. All my life, I was always called to doing something in sales but I either self-sabotaged or created an excuse; I settled for being an employee and being the best for someone else. I thrived when it came to working for someone else but always failed when I would have to do it for myself.

I didn't realize, that day when I got my results, that my then naive interpretation of those results was going to have a negative impact on me for so many years, and would keep me misaligned with my true purpose. My misconception and the cringing feeling I felt in my stomach any time I would mention the word "sales" kept me from thriving and finding success in positions that I could have thrived in and excelled.

But back then, there was no one to educate me on the benefits and the gift it was to be great in sales. Now, there are colleges that teach the art of sales to people. There are programs and books, like "The Psychology of Selling" by Denis Waitley, that are an excellent resource. As I look back, I realized how easily it was for me to build relationships with people—it was very natural. I lived the by the principles I learned in "How to Win Friends and Influence People" by Dale Carnegie.

In my last chapter, I mentioned how I transitioned from one job to another, from a Paraeducator to a sales rep at a large telecommunications company. When I think back to when I was leaving the school district, I recall the feeling of dread and embarrassment mentioning that I was leaving to go into sales. I didn't know it at the time, but the sense of dread came from fear of my own perception that I had about salespeople.

I never wanted to consider myself a "salesperson," because, for me, salespeople in these positions didn't have a great reputation. I personally never recall having a great experience of my own when it came to purchasing phones, wondering what are they going to stick me with now; are they being honest? Unfortunately, once I started the job, I realized I wasn't the only one that felt this way.

This actually became a window of opportunity for me, as I realized quickly that I was good at building rapport and gaining people's trust and therefore excelled in sales. This was an opportunity to give people sales in this industry under a new light. And for me, it was a great opportunity to make a difference and step into and embrace and own my power as leader of sales and of relationships.

Because that is actually what sales is: relationships—and I thrived in this. For many years, I was the buyer—now, I sell with pride, confidence, and integrity that aligns with my values. My friend Dr. Chibu said it best: In life, there two types of people in a relationship: a buyer and a seller— which do you choose to be?"

What this experience taught me was that my perception of what others, including myself, thought about salespeople created a misalignment with my ability to make more money. Not being aligned with sales made it difficult for me to find success in running a business, because you can't have a business if you can't sell, or don't choose to sell. My prejudice towards selling because of my perception of how I thought others viewed sales reps made me lose money and created a lack of confidence, which prevented me from showing up as the true leader that I am.

I have always been very good at following my intuitive directions. In November of 2023, I followed my intuition and decided to take a job in sales. I know for a fact that this feeling and opportunity was coming to me from a higher power—God, to be exact. I wasn't thrilled with the idea at first, but I took action, and I am so glad I did. Trusting the process took me down a path of self-discovery and bringing in alignment with what was always in me. That was the lesson here, not allowing the fear and judgment to continue to rule and prevent me from my true purpose.

All those years, the knowing but not taking action kept me stuck. Success truly is facing whatever makes us uncomfortable and finding answers because, when we do, we also find breakthroughs. Denis Whitley mentioned in his book, "The Psychology of Selling," only successful people are the 20 percent of the 20/80 rule when it comes to selling.

Three months in sales, I was at the top and still growing. I realized that the art of sales came to me easily and effortlessly—all I had to do was embrace it. I know now that this gift is part of my identity and how I serve others. It's not the product that sells—it's me and my relationship with others that sells, so I can sell anything as long as it's in alignment with my values. What made people love me and trust me was my integrity.

Not being aligned with the word "salesperson" and my perception of feeling uncomfortable also made me feel inadequate as a business owner, causing me to fail. I mean, as a business owner, to stay in business you need to sell, so feeling misaligned with selling negatively impacted my business and as a person.

We buy into what people sell us, whether it be their products, stories, or relationships, and vice versa. We are always selling or buying through relationships.

FATIMA HURD

About Fatima Hurd: In addition to her professional achievements, Fatima Hurd is also a talented photographer who has a passion for working with and photographing female entrepreneurs. She believes in the power of visual storytelling and understands the importance of showcasing authenticity in front of the camera. Fatima's photography sessions with female entrepreneurs are not just about capturing beautiful images, but also about empowering them to show up authentically. She creates a safe and supportive environment where her clients can feel comfortable being themselves and expressing their unique personalities and stories. Through her photography, Fatima aims to capture the essence and spirit of each individual she works with. She believes that by showcasing the authentic selves of female entrepreneurs, she can help them build a strong personal brand and connect with their target audience on a deeper level.

Fatima's diverse skill set as an OBA Coach, certified hypnotherapist, Best-Selling Author, and photographer allows her to provide a holistic approach to empowering and supporting female entrepreneurs. She understands the challenges they face in both their personal and professional lives and is dedicated to helping them overcome obstacles and achieve their goals. With her passion for helping others and her commitment to making a positive impact in the world, Fatima Hurd is not only a successful professional but also a role model for women who aspire to live authentically and make a difference in their own lives and the lives of others.

Author's Website: *www.FatimaHurd.com*

Book Series Website: *www.ThePrinciplesOfDebbieAndGoliath.com*

JOANNA JAMES
FINDING ALIGNMENT THROUGH ADJUSTING YOUR FOCUS

"The successful warrior is the average man, with laser-like focus."
~ **Bruce Lee**

My Darling Self

Welcome to the revelation that your focus and alignment are intricately interrelated. As you find your alignment in life, you will have to adjust your focus. Similarly, without being in alignment, it is very difficult to maintain your focus. It's one of life's practical jokes, like the proverbial question of which came first: the chicken or the egg? To make sense of it, you will need to ponder: Where does your focus originate from?

Understanding Focus: Your Internal Spotlight

Focus is the magical ability to maintain your concentration while tuning out the rest of the world's noise. Think of it as your internal spotlight, illuminating the path to your dreams or what I call your ultimate focus. Having the vision or foresight of what you want is just the first part of the puzzle. The real art is maintaining persistent action as you move towards it. Depending on what that is, it may require short bursts of your attention, or it may take years of dedication. This, of course, requires the art of concentration, and concentration requires deep practice and patience.

The Challenge of Modern Distractions

The speed at which the world is changing is accelerating exponentially. The craft of developing one's concentration will soon be lost to the war of distraction. Your environment is built upon the relentless pursuit of information stimulation, creating a dopamine nation hooked on the white noise of distraction. In the future, addiction will take a new form, one generated internally by external parties. You must beware the pitfalls of a distracted mind, for your mind is not your friend. If you are not the one commanding its direction, your life will never be your own. To start your training, you must first defend yourself against distractions at all costs.

Strengthening Your Focus Muscle

There will be times when you realize that your focus has drifted. This type of distraction is only natural; we all experience it. Just like a muscle, you will need to strengthen your resolve while you encounter the variation of thoughts your mind will present to you in order to maintain your mental focus upon the object of your desire.

Life's Detours and Distractions

Life itself is full of detours, some positive and some not. Your mind is the generator of these experiences. Both varieties can form distractions from the pursuit of your dreams (your ultimate focus). When these distractions accumulate, you will certainly find yourself falling out of alignment. Life may become difficult, demanding, or take an undesirable form.

Harnessing the Power of Reflection

This is when you will need to harness the power of reflection. Reflection is like looking into the mirror of your soul. It allows you to see where you are and, more importantly, where you have deviated off track. This is the key moment when you must adjust your course. You see, when you are out of alignment, it is a sign that your focus has been interrupted— certainly from the positive things that you truly want.

Embracing Change and Adaptability

The only constant in life is change, and so be mindful that your changing thoughts are a part of the natural course of things. Just as the sea ebbs and flows, the moon waxes and wanes, so too will your focus. The sooner you embrace it, the smoother your journey will be. Your flexibility and adaptability are key to maintaining focus; simply adjust your sails and continue moving forward.

Where we too often fail is with the voice of self-criticism and doubt that appears during these moments of transition. Far better to accept that you are off course and adjust—the rest is just another distraction designed to keep you further off track. With the passage of time, you will find that your ability to stay true to the course you chart will improve, and you will learn the early signs of a storm when one is brewing, just as you will find the fortitude to travel through them.

Learning from Setbacks

Realize that setbacks are not failures; each one carries a lesson, and by learning from them, you become wiser. Wisdom is a wonderful thing—in fact, one of life's most valuable treasures—so use that knowledge to realign your efforts in the direction you wish to now set. It is in this process of realignment, when we adapt our focus back onto what we truly want, that we create the sense of alignment again. Just like a ship, our focus is the compass and the rudder is our alignment; both must work together to arrive at the destination.

The Continuous Process of Alignment

As you embark on this journey of finding alignment, remember that it is a continuous process of adapting and adjusting your focus. Energy flows where your attention goes, so keep your mind on what you want and off the things you don't. You shape your destiny by the small moments of sustained focus.

The Power of Sustained Focus

It is said we typically overestimate what can be achieved in one year and underestimate what can be done in ten. This very example serves to show us the power of sustained focus. As Robert Collier said, "Success is the sum of small efforts, repeated day in and day out."

The Symbiotic Nature of Focus and Alignment

The truly magical part of the journey is when you are in alignment and clear about your focus. You have an internal generator that expedites the journey. The symbiotic nature serves to propel the ship faster. The interwoven nature of it all is truly divine. You see, to create alignment, you must consider your focus, and to maintain your focus you must consider your alignment.

Practical Tools for Your Journey

To assist you with your journey, here are three simple tools to practice:

1. **Daily Journaling:** Spend 5 minutes each evening journaling about your day. Write down anything that comes to mind, especially anything disturbing to the mind, so you can choose to let it dissipate while you sleep.
2. **Mindfulness Meditation:** Dedicate 5 minutes each morning to mindfulness meditation. Focus on your breath and bring your attention back whenever it wanders.
3. **Declutter Your Space:** Remove all unnecessary or broken items to create a clean, distraction-free environment.

P.S. Remember to remove as many distractions from your life as possible. Your focus and alignment are your greatest allies on this journey. Keep them sharp, and you will navigate through life with clarity and purpose.

JOANNA JAMES

About Joanna James: Joanna James is known as a revolutionary difference maker in the Design, Construction, and Banking sectors and is featured in publications such as Entrepreneur, USA Today, The Advisor, MPA, Australian Broker, Flaunt, CIO, and Insights Success.

As Australia's youngest registered female architect and builder, she is known as creator of the world's first 'Bio' home, featured on TV series 'I Own Australia's Best Home.'

Joanna created the Shambhala@byron retreat which welcomed celebrity singer Sting as her first guest. Her book *Mind Body Spaces* raises awareness around our health and the spaces that we live in. A pioneering entrepreneur for the Mortgage Ezy Group of companies, her contribution shines through the 32 Industry awards including 3 times BRW fastest company.

A passionate advocate for women in business, Joanna has also been recognized as Principal of the Year (WIFA), Top 100 Female Entrepreneurs, and Top 100 Female Mentors. Contributing to the FBAA Artemis Forum, she works to raise opportunities for Education, Advocacy, and Awareness for women within the Australian Finance Industry.

Author's Website: *www.JoannaJames.com*

Book Series Website: *www.ThePrinciplesOfDebbieAndGoliath.com*

KATHERINE VARGAS
AMAZING GRACE

. . . .

"Little girl, I say to you, get up!"
~ Mark 5:41

My name is Katherine, and I am one of God's chosen surrogate mothers. What does that mean? That means I am a mother to three beautiful children, but only one living child.

When I was seventeen years old, I saw my niece being born. My mother lied and told the hospital I was eighteen so I could stay in the room while my older sister was in labor. I saw the natural birth of my niece and from then on, I vowed I would not have children; that was too traumatizing. Fast forward about thirteen years later, and all I wanted was to become a mother.

I went the traditional route, met a man, fell in love, was married two years later, had a big wedding. We bought a condo and waited a few months to have a child. I am Mexican, so I thought it would be incredibly easy to get pregnant. I was wrong. After about a year of trial and error, $500+ of acupuncture, and after a complete surrender to God, I was finally pregnant.

I had already dreamed that I would have my little girl Marina, named after my best friend, my grandma Marina. Marina is my perfect little peanut. Small but mighty in every way. I refer to her as my "spicy peanut" due to her sassiness and small stature. God gave me the perfect gift in 2018—He gave me her.

January 2020 arrived; strange things were happening in the world. Although there was so much uncertainty, my husband and I decided to take a risk, sell our condo, and move to our "Dream city," the one we really wanted to raise a family in but was nowhere in reach for us financially.

Fortunately, my Godfather helped us find the cheapest home in the nicest neighborhood. Everything was looking up when the world was falling apart. We bought our house and began turning it into our home: we loved our neighbors, I was back in school to obtain my Master's, and I was ready to start a side gig as a mobile Notary for extra income. In my mind, 2021 was looking prosperous for us!

October of 2020, we learned I was pregnant. I thought, "What a perfect age gap for Marina and her future sibling." We were thrilled. I just had to keep it a secret a little longer. December 2020, I went to my appointment ready to hear the heartbeat. Unfortunately, I didn't.

I was 9 weeks pregnant, and the doctors somehow estimated I miscarried at around 7 weeks. I tried to pass the baby naturally, but the baby did not want to leave my body. If I waited any longer, I would risk my own life.

After a few days, the doctor finally ordered me to go to the ER. The male doctor handed me two pills. One to take at the hospital and one to take home. He told me I would experience some "light cramping" and it would be over.

I took the pill, went home, and within a few hours I was crying in the fetal position experiencing the worst physical and psychological pain I had ever experienced in my life. My husband told my daughter I was sick, and he tried to put her to bed so I could pass our child in the bathroom without her knowing. I just remember laying in the shower, crying for what seemed like forever, exhausted, and defeated. Eventually, it was over. My little Ruby was gone.

I sat in grief for weeks. The holidays were so hard to enjoy with fears of Covid and trying not to have an emotional breakdown in front of my family. I dropped out of school, stopped my notary training, and just grieved. I didn't have the motivation anymore. I didn't have the same goals I had just two months prior. My fire was out.

At the same time, I had my daughter Marina. She was in this very fun age. She was so inquisitive, so in tune with my emotions and feelings. She still needed mommy and mommy needed to get it together. I remember at one point reading this story in the Bible about how this little girl's parents went to Jesus and begged Him to heal her. She was dead. Jesus went to the girl's lifeless body, took her hand, and said "Talithia koum!" which means, "Little girl, I say to you, get up!"

When I read that, I felt it so deep in my soul. I felt like I was that little lifeless girl, and He was telling me, get up! I'm here now, you're fine, get up, little girl. So, I did. Although the pandemic was not fully over, I told my husband I needed to go back to church in person. I needed to heal from this pain. We began attending in person church, I joined one of the group studies, and I began therapy.

Within a few months, I shifted my focus on health and healing rather than education and career planning. I started becoming vulnerable. I started asking for help. Although I did "get up", I wasn't strong just yet but knew I could get there again. I began to eat better and exercise. I gained energy and strength. I needed it, especially when I found out my niece was pregnant, and her due date was my Ruby's due date (in July). I felt like God was telling me she needed me now the way I needed her when my daughter was born. It was a painful request, but I was so excited over this new blessing.

A few weeks later, I found out I was pregnant again. I attribute that pregnancy to my "health journey." I was in this women's fitness group called 'Grit and Grace' so I thought it would be cute, if I was pregnant with a girl, to name her Grace. Due to my age at this point, and the fact that I had a miscarriage a few months earlier, I had to see a high-risk specialist.

I was so impatient; I went without my husband to that appointment. The ultrasound tech came in, she showed me the baby and then the best part… I heard the heartbeat! Nice and loud. I had these thick warm tears streaming down my face and over my smile. I could not contain my excitement and relief anymore; that heartbeat was music to my ears. The ultrasound tech gave me a tissue, told me to sit tight until the doctor can review the images and advised me he would be in shortly. I laid back in pure bliss, thanking God profusely.

The doctor came in, introduced himself, and let me know he reviewed the ultrasound. He put the images on a screen for me and pointed at the back of the baby's head and said, "This is my concern." Once he said those words, I went into complete shock and panic. Everything he said after I needed him to repeat because I couldn't process anything he was trying to explain to me. I told him I just had a miscarriage, and I couldn't take anymore bad news. He explained that there was too much fluid behind the baby's neck and that I could undergo genetic testing. He would set up a meeting with a genetic counselor for more information.

I went to my car and cried hot tears of anger. I called my husband and could hardly speak. He later told me that when I called him, he thought the baby was dead already, just from the way I was crying. He hung up and headed home immediately. I called my best friend, Teresa, who had a very similar story in 2015: she made the decision to terminate her pregnancy after multiple appointments of only bad news. She was the first person to tell me, "Do not abort the baby, you will regret it, you can do this."

I hung up with her and called my mother. I could hardly breathe, but I had to get to the lab to begin these tests so I drove to the lab while my mother told me, "God won't give you what you can't handle." Again, it was nothing I wanted to hear. I could not fathom losing another child; I felt like I was being punished for something. I went to the lab, had my first of many blood draws, and went home to cry.

The next day, we met with the genetic counselor; we answered a series of questions about both sides of our family medical history. No one on either side had genetic disorders. She then went through the possibilities of which genetic disorder we were looking at, but they were all under the "Trisomy" umbrella which meant the baby had three copies of chromosomes instead of two.

After weeks of testing and waiting extra weeks for results, we were mentally and emotionally battling over what was the best course of action, all the while my baby was growing inside of me. On the final decision day, I asked if I could see her one more time on the ultrasound before we made our decision. The doctor, who at this point was frustrated that we wouldn't just terminate her, left the room. The ultrasound tech turned on the machine and we saw her, and this little girl waved at us. She waved, like she was asking for our mercy and strength. We decided to keep her, the doctor referred us elsewhere to continue treatment (I guess we were no longer worth his time), and we prepared to have a child with Trisomy 18, a fetal fatal diagnosis.

Here is the long story short: we had an army of support around us because, through therapy, we learned to be vulnerable and ask for help and seek help. We prepared our daughter Marina as much as possible; we told her that she was a big sister—however, her little sister was chosen by God to be a princess in the kingdom of heaven.

I wanted to announce my pregnancy (because everyone could eventually tell I was pregnant) and I wanted to explain what was next. I posted about her on social media, letting everyone know, yes, I was pregnant, however due to her fetal fatal diagnosis we were not bringing her home. Instead, I encouraged everyone to send a gift to a local pregnancy center in Huntington Beach under the name "Grace Vargas" in her honor. This pregnancy center received about 60 packages in about one month from that post. The pregnancy center thanked us by bringing us in as a family to introduce Marina to her little sister via 4D Ultrasound.

I joined a Trisomy 18 support group on Facebook. I made friends with other trisomy moms, both through that group and through other mutual friends. The hard truth was hitting us hard as we realized that her odds were against us. Our friends had their baby in November, and she died 9 days later. We were due in December. The week she was due, I was a mess. We changed her birth plan to be a scheduled c-section so it would be less stressful on her body. December 9th was Marina's Christmas recital at school. We watched her nervously on stage. We ate dinner as a family, and we sent her off with my mother-in-law for the night.

December 10th, very early in the morning, we headed to the hospital. The staff at the new hospital treated us like VIP from the minute we were referred to them (we still keep in touch with our fetal care coordinator). They had her birth plan; they knew she would not see the NICU but only be in our arms the entire time. We had the C-section not knowing if she would live through it, but then we heard this miraculous little sound of a kitten, and that kitten was our three-pound miracle baby girl, Grace.

Our family and friends flooded our room over the next four days: Marina got to meet her sister, we had photos, prayers, and lots of hope! I remember just holding her, begging God to let me keep her. The doctors and nurses in general labor and delivery loved checking her because they were only used to seeing babies that small in the NICU. She was thriving on her own.

They sent us home after four days. Our family and church had quickly gathered micro-preemie items for us to take her home. The reality was, we were also going home with a triage team. The reality was, she still had trisomy. We tried to enjoy our time with her, anyway. Marina was a proud big sister and we were so happy to have had decorated before we went to the hospital so the girls could truly experience Christmas together. Christmas came and went; we saw very few family members because we did not want to expose the girls to any virus during our time together. It was still the best Christmas our little family had ever had. We had gifts and food delivered to our door every day. We called our family through video chats.

I remember being on video chat with Grace and my cousin Ronald. He was battling cancer at the time, and he was such a huge support throughout my miscarriage and through Grace's journey. Introducing them to each other via chat will forever hold a special memory in my heart.

A few days later, on December 28th, we learned some of our family members had COVID. We made sure to stay home and still just enjoy our time. My mother did come to pick up Marina, who, at this point, needed a break from being home. My husband worked in the garage to prevent draft from entering the house. I sat on the couch with my sleepy Grace bundled on my chest.

My husband came in the house, and I asked him to hold Grace so I could make tea. The next thing I knew, he was in a panic, taking her temperature and asking me to call 911. She was dying in his arms. I think she was waiting for him specifically to take her final breath. She had already had time with her sister, she had her time with me, she was just waiting to say goodbye to her daddy. So, she did.

One would think that losing your child is the worst thing in the world 1, and it is. I do not recommend it to anyone! However, through faith, work, community and internal healing... This little girl got back up. God chose me not only to be a surrogate mother, but to share Grace's journey and the goodness and eternal impact she made not only in my life, but the lives of others as well.

I am now a parent education advocate for Horizon Pregnancy Clinic, and my husband and I have sat with quite a few families who have gone through or are going through similar journeys. Marina processes death as something both beautiful and sad, which is a healthier way than I ever processed death as a child or adult. Through us, Grace's legacy will live on, and I will continue to be a mom of three with my one (spicy) living and loving child.

KATHERINE VARGAS

About Katherine Vargas: Katherine Vargas is a dedicated and experienced professional specializing in the field of notary and loan signing services. Based in Orange County, CA, Katherine has established herself as a reliable Mobile Notary and Loan Signing Agent, known for her meticulous attention to detail and commitment to delivering top-quality service. Beyond her notary expertise, she is also recognized as a skilled Small Business Networking & Marketing Coach, where she leverages her extensive knowledge to help small businesses thrive in competitive markets.

Her expertise extends to legal intake, showcasing her versatility and comprehensive understanding of the legal aspects intertwined with her professional endeavors.

Katherine's website, *www.MrsKatherineVargas.com*, serves as a gateway for clients to access her services and benefit from her vast experience. Her proficiency, combined with her dedication to client satisfaction, makes her an invaluable asset to anyone seeking expert notary services, loan signing assistance, and business marketing coaching.

Author's Website: *www.MrsKatherineVargas.com*

Book Series Website: *www.ThePrinciplesOfDebbieAndGoliath.com*

> The future belongs to those who believe in the beauty of their dreams.
>
> ~ Eleanor Roosevelt

KATIE MARES

RISING ABOVE: MY JOURNEY OF VISION, ACTION, & FOCUS AS A SURVIVOR

My name is Katie, and my story is one of resilience and redemption. I survived domestic abuse, a storm that left me shattered and broken. I was thrown away like yesterday's news, my credit cards canceled, my bank accounts frozen. I was told to sell my body for groceries, a cruel taunt that still haunts me.

I cried tears of despair, feeling lost and alone, for five days. But then, in the depths of my despair, something shifted within me. I made a choice —a choice to take control of my life and reclaim my power. With steely determination, I wiped away my tears and stood tall, ready to face whatever challenges lay ahead. My new not for profit was conceived on day 5: Ladies Take Control. It is an organization focused on inspiring women to find the courage to do hard things, regardless of their circumstances, knowing that rising from the depths of darkness is a choice and they have the power in them to do so.

Rebuilding my life seemed like an impossible task, but I refused to let fear hold me back. I knew I had to take action, no matter how small, to move forward. And so, with each passing day, I took deliberate steps towards my goals, refusing to let the scars of my past define my future.

Focus became my guiding light, a beacon of hope in the darkness. I honed my attention on my dreams, blocking out distractions and naysayers along the way. Through mindfulness practices and daily rituals, I cultivated a sense of clarity and purpose that propelled me forward, even when the road ahead seemed daunting.

As a single mother, I faced challenges that would have seemed insurmountable to many. I even gave up my food so they could eat, but I refused to be defined by my circumstances. Instead, I embraced my role as a survivor, using my past experiences to fuel my determination to succeed.

With each passing day, my confidence grew, and my once-shattered dreams began to take shape before my eyes. I found myself stepping into a new career, rebuilding my life from the ground up with resilience and grace.

My story is not just my own; it is a testament to the power that lies within each and every woman to rise above adversity and create a life of purpose and meaning. It is a reminder that no matter how dark the night may seem, there is always hope on the horizon, waiting to be embraced.

So, to all the women out there who dare to dream, I say this: Embrace your vision with courage and conviction, take consistent action in pursuit of your goals, and focus your energies on what truly matters. Within you lies the power to overcome any obstacle and achieve your wildest dreams. You are stronger than you know, and you are capable of greatness beyond measure.

With love and boundless belief in your potential,

XO,

Katie

KATIE MARES

About Katie Mares: As a brand experience expert, Katie knows firsthand the challenges organizations encounter as they strive to design a sustainable and effective CX program tailored for the female consumer. Using her experiences as a Chief Inspiration Officer, building company infrastructure and designing customer experience programs, she is now a leading voice for positive, actionable change in the organizations with which she partners. Katie has a Master's degree in Adult Training and Development from Schulich School of Business and a Certified Training and Development Professional (CTDP) certification. As a highly sought-after speaker, Katie has inspired audiences around the world to think differently about the female consumer, customer experience, and leadership. She has worked with globally recognized brands, including Honda, Celebrity Cruises, and Canada Post.

Katie lives in Toronto with her three children. When she is not traveling around the world consulting and speaking, she can be found on a yoga mat, in a shoe store, or snuggled on the couch eating homemade popcorn and watching a movie with her three little ones.

Author's Website: *www.KatieMares.com*

Book Series Website: *www.ThePrinciplesOfDebbieAndGoliath.com*

LAUREN COBB

FINDING ALIGNMENT DURING MY TEENAGE ERA

When I was a teen, there was a boy who I was introduced to and we instantly became such good friends. He was outgoing and funny; we had a lot in common. We spent every day at school together along with other friends of ours. Throughout the next five years, we stayed close friends.

We did a lot of things as a friend group. We went to local youth dances together with our friends, and we went on dates off and on but mostly were just friends. He was a very religious kid; he held himself to very high standards, which I respected. He chose not to kiss anyone until after high school. He and his cousin, who also went to school with us, had a pact that they wouldn't ever go on two dates in a row with the same girl to keep them from being tempted to pursue her more. It was a little overboard in my opinion, but I respected it. We were able to build a SOLID friendship throughout those years, one I still cherish to this day.

I was comfortable around boys because I had 6 older brothers who had friends who were around all the time. I also had high standards compared to most of my peers, however, as I dated a lot and had some boyfriends throughout my teenage years. I was a tease and LOVED to tease/flirt with the boys.

One of the boys who I became close to was VERY different from the usual group I hung around with. He had a ROUGH childhood. Parents on drugs, while kids were put into the foster system at a very young age. At

127

times, he would get to go be with family for a while and then back into the system he and his siblings went. When I met him, he had been with his current family for a few years and was being adopted by them. They were a great family who had older children of their own and then fostered and adopted 2 more sets of siblings who were all close to the same age.

He was a great kid, and had a ROUGH time finding himself but meant well. He treated me very well. Because we lived so far apart, we didn't get to see each other more than a couple times a month. Our relationship lasted a few years throughout high school. When we spent time together, it was often with his family or my friends.

His group of friends was a rough crowd! His mom encouraged our dating because she was hopeful that it would influence him to be better—which it did do. We spent many hours talking on the phone, emailing back and forth and chatting on MSN Messenger. (I guess I am showing my age now! There was no texting then!) When we were together, we had fun: horseback riding, and we loved to go paint balling and play night games. He was SO much fun to be around. We laughed ALL THE TIME.

Over the years, it started to wear on me. When we were apart, he would often get into trouble at school, with friends, cause problems at home, and overall didn't have the confidence to stand alone and be a better person and not let his peers influence him. He eventually got sent to a juvenile detention center for a while. It was hard. He would call and we would have conversations and he would be in tears talking about how he wished he could change, how I made him want to do better.

This always caused a conflict inside me. I cared SO much for him and he treated ME so well, respected my values and never tried to push me to do things he knew were wrong. We were dating but we weren't exclusive. I went on many dates and spent more in-person time with the other group of friends I talked about above.

If you've followed along with other book series, I am sure you have heard me talk about my schooling experience. I attended a religious private school, which was structured into franchises. I attended the main school in Salt Lake City, UT. The original school and headquarters were here.

I was also a Student Body Officer in middle school and went on to be National Student Body Vice President and then National Student Body President. I was widely known in this community and so was my boyfriend… but for different reasons. Everyone knew of our friendship and many would comment and not always kind things and OFTEN these were adults in my life making comments.

One summer at a Youth Conference hosted by our school, specifically planned and hosted by the Student Government, he came along with his parents. We were on day 2 of 4 and we had been out hiking, playing outdoor games, and swimming in the lake. It had been a long day. We wrapped up the day and we all had some free time after dinner and then we all were sent to our separate lodging.

That night, we were all just goofing off in the girls' lodging, and so I went outside and down the road a little to say hi to my boyfriend and his family. We were sitting outside the RV and, after a while, we all went inside the RV because the bugs were getting bad. At this point, someone noticed I was missing from the girls' lodging. So, the adults came looking and, of course, they knew where to go look first.

I remember Mr. Nicoles coming to the door and yelling "Is Lauren inside here?" He immediately assumed they were "hiding" me in there to be with my boyfriend. I went out and he still kept going on about things. He claimed to believe me. Life went on for the week. It was a great week! My parents came to pick me up, along with a handful of other kids. It was a 3-hour drive home. I could tell my mom was acting off. So, me being me, I kept asking if everything was okay.

Finally, she just let it out. She let me have it! Apparently, after that night, I was with the family in the RV, and that leader went back and called my parents… but instead of just telling them what happened he embellished it A LOT, and then on the day of pick up, others felt it was necessary to add to the story. I was being accused of sneaking off MULTIPLE times during the day as well and making out with him by the basketball court and all kinds of things. It was bizarre. My mom believed it all. Why? Because of the kind of person this boy "was."

Still, to this day, it hurts my heart to think about all the assumptions made but specifically about him. Things eventually got sorted out for me. I didn't lose my position in student government and didn't even get a slap on the wrists. Turns out, when you have friends and you're in a big group nearly the whole time people can't get away with making things up and, also, there wasn't even a basketball court on the property we were at!

Fast forward a year or so from that point, and I had some choices to make. He wasn't going forward in life and I had some big opportunities ahead. I had to decide what mental baggage I could carry and what I couldn't. Although I had kept going forward and doing amazing things throughout those years we were together, I couldn't ever put my whole heart into something new because I felt a need to hold space for him. I felt a need to always be there for him when he needed to vent and needed to be reminded that he wouldn't have to be defined by these choices his whole life.

It was a heavy thing to carry, yet I couldn't let it go. It took some time, but right before I left on my third study-abroad trip to the Middle East, I was turning 18 that summer and I knew I had to let go. I could not be that person for him anymore. As much as it hurt, I had to say goodbye. It was a hard day; I remember it vividly still. I HAD to move my focus and be fully aligned with my goals and desires. Always being tied to his emotional trauma was not going to allow me to fully move forward in my life.

That day was hard and I had to be 100% transparent and honest with him. We had YEARS of friendship, trust, and love for each other that was unconditional. But I knew I couldn't be ALL THAT for him anymore. That day ended with not even a real hug goodbye. It was SO hard on me. Hard on him too, I know. Sadly, it isn't a story of him finally deciding to make some real hard changes and coming back around clean and living a great life. But, for me, it was heartache but freeing.

Thanks to my friend who I mentioned in the very beginning of this chapter, I had support and encouragement to follow my intuition and go for my dreams and people who were not judging me throughout the years but were always there to remind me of my focus and potential. He'd listen to my struggles and heartache of my boyfriend who was so up and down but never once judged me for sticking with my boyfriend.

He would ask how my boyfriend was and empathize and then talk to me about my life and goals and while my dreams that summer and following year did not go 100% or even 50% of what I had envisioned at the time. I decided to end things with my boyfriend, and I was able to be in a spot where I met my now husband and that summer Ty and I met. We were on a study abroad and came home and got to teach youth leadership conferences together and my life surely leveled up and into alignment with what I knew my potential is. This ultimately has landed me here where I am today. I wouldn't have it any other way!

The top things I learned from those years include:

Never be afraid to be YOU. I was always upfront about my standards and my goals in life with my teenage boyfriend. We lived two very different lives and not once did I fall into his way of life, but he also knew where I stood and knew he couldn't change that. That was part of what drew him to me!

Don't give in to others who try to derail you. FOCUS! That teacher who tried to throw me under the bus at that youth conference showed his true colors and while I wanted to be SO mad, I chose to not give into the "he said, she said" of things and thankfully had friends who knew me well enough that stood up for me as well. Things ended up in my favor as I was able to hold my head up and continue with life while things were sorted out and decisions were being made about my future with student government. Had I been booted off the team, I would not have had the opportunity to pursue my study abroad programs and leadership teaching.

Don't push others aside just because they aren't just like you. If I had pushed my friend aside because of his HIGH standards as a teen, I would not have had the support and counsel during those years.

Be true to yourself. A.K.A Alignment! Had I let someone else's emotional baggage hold space in my heart and brain at that time in life, I would not have had the focus to pursue my dreams that I knew were in alignment with what I wanted for my future.

> *"When the basis for your actions is inner alignment with the present moment, Your actions become empowered by the intelligence of life itself."*
> ~ Eckhart Tolle

LAUREN COBB

About Lauren Cobb: Lauren Cobb is a wife to her amazing and supportive husband Tyler. A mother to 3 beautiful daughters who've taught her more in the last 12 years than she has learned in the first 23 years of her life.

At a young age Lauren knew she had a lot of ambition and drive. As she became an adult, she knew that entrepreneurship was her passion and thankfully married someone who supported that! Together with Ty they own a graphic and media design company that they've built from the ground up. Growing and seeing the successes from their own efforts has been one of the most rewarding experiences!

Self-development and leadership have been a big part of Lauren's life since she was 14. She traveled and taught leadership to youth across the country throughout her high school years. She knows first-hand how self-development is crucial to success in life. Knowing who you are and finding your purpose and passion is important.

As Lauren and her husband Ty are building their businesses and seeking a network and friends who are aligned with their values, they've found in Champion Circle and learned how to properly mastermind. Lauren is a member of the corporate executive team at Champion Circle Networking Association, founded and led by Jon Kovach Jr. Masterminds have changed her life and their business for the better.

Author's Website: *www.TyCobb.MyPortfolio.com*

Book Series Website: *www.ThePrinciplesOfDebbieAndGoliath.com*

133

.

LIZ SEARS

MULTIPLY RESULTS—LIVE AN AMAZING LIFE

How often are you asked, "What do you want to be when you grow up?" I swear I was asked that question a hundred times as a kid, but one time one of my favorite teachers had us write down what our dream job would look like. And this changed everything for me.

I think I was about 15 years old, and as I sat in my classroom hearing the clock ticking, I began to imagine. Hmm, what do I want? Well, I love people and being social, so I want a job where I meet new people often. And I get bored sitting at a desk all day, so I definitely want to be able to come and go during the day. I like feeling important, so I want to have important conversations about important things and a great office with a mini fridge full of my favorite drinks. I like to be helpful and to share things I know, so that needs to be part of what I do, and I'm a total math and debate nerd so it would be super cool if I could have numbers and legal stuff be part of what I do.

And I wanted to earn a LOT of money! I grew up in humble circumstances with eleven siblings (I know! Crazy, right?) so extra money was non-existent. If I wanted money to buy lotion, school clothes, or just a hamburger from McDonald's, I had to earn it. So, starting at 12-years-old, I babysat and did other odd jobs to earn my spending cash. This is why earning a lot of money was important to me. I wanted to grow up and be able to buy whatever I wanted and help whoever I could.

After writing down all the parts of my dream job, I turned in the assignment. Fast forward 20 years. I'm in my basement, going through old papers from school and I run across this assignment. I sit on the floor in that crowded storage room full of boxes and old books, and I read the words I'd written down. Whoa! I had created exactly that, even down to the mini fridge! I am a Realtor with a small, successful team. I meet new people all the time. I help them with the biggest purchase of their lives; I help them with something as important as where their family calls home! I earn a great income and I get to work with numbers and contracts. I also get to work both in an office and around town. It's so fun!

Fast forward another 14 years, and I've been able to build upon it even more.

The best part of what I do now is helping others to design and create a life they love! In the first book of this series, I share my 21-Day Dream Challenge to create your Life Plan.

In this book, I share 3 ways to Focus and Align your life. First, how to empower yourself to use your Life Plan as a guide. Second, how to avoid pitfalls that are disguised as good advice. And third, how to multiply your results by inspiring those around you.

Part 1: Empower Yourself

The first step to empowerment is to own your role as the lead character in your life. You are the *hero* in your story! It's so easy sometimes to feel stuck with everything you "have to do," but I'm going to let you in on a secret. You don't "have" to do anything. Instead, you decide what you want and "choose" actions to achieve it. Like, I hate doing laundry, but I like having the things I want to wear, clean and easy to find.

Essentially, everything I "have" to do either creates a result I want or helps me avoid a consequence I don't want. Take a moment and think about each thing you feel like you "have" to do and notice if it's a result you are trying to create or a consequence you want to avoid. Once you realize that you don't "have" to do anything, the key is to identify what results you want, and then "choose" actions to achieve them. I call it "behave for the result you want."

This is a mantra I'll say in my head when I am feeling stuck. I'll think, "Liz, behave for the result you want. What do you want?" And then I will take time to answer the question. The clearer I am on what I want, the easier it is to want to act. It almost feels a bit like a superpower because of how it shifts my energy!

This is where your Life Plan comes into play. You've already identified what you want. If you review your Life Plan regularly, it can keep your focus clear so that you make the best choices to get you where you want to go. At least once a year, review and update your life plan to keep it in line with your changing circumstances and growth.

Part 2: Avoid Pitfalls

As girls and women today, we are often fed lies that undermine our power and sabotage our resourcefulness and creativity. Recognizing all of the resources available to you as well as recognizing bad advice will help you avoid pitfalls.

When I wrote my dream job assignment, it was about 1990. Just 16 years before that, in 1974, women weren't allowed to get a credit card without a man co-signing on the credit application. Just a few decades before that, women struggled to get a job outside the home without a man's approval. And before 1920, women weren't even allowed to vote. But in 1990, none of those barriers existed and I knew I could do anything I wanted.

Today, some women teach young girls that they are still victims of situations that haven't existed in decades. This is one of the lies that is being taught. Some women teach that men want to hold you back and treat you unfairly. This is another lie that is being taught. While some situations create barriers to your dreams and some men may treat you unfairly, these are uncommon and can be overcome when you know what to look for and how to respond.

First, here's what to look for. Look for *solutions*, not problems. Look for women who have overcome similar holdbacks to what you're facing and how they did it. Look for good men and women who want to help you succeed because I promise you, there are way more people who want to see you succeed than those who want to hold you back.

Second, here's how to respond. Be gracious to those who want to hold you back or who treat you unfairly. There is power in recognizing that everyone behaves in a way that makes perfect sense based on what they know, their past experiences, what's currently happening in their lives, and how they see the world. This includes you. Be gracious to everyone, even if they're wrong. Their opinion doesn't matter when it comes to your goals. And sometimes what appears as a setback at first turns out to be a launchpad. So be kind, let it go, and expect to find solutions. Then behave for the result you want.

If you want to be respected, behave respectably. If you want to be promoted at work, earn it by doing more work and better work than you're paid for. If you want great friendships, be a great friend. You won't always get the exact result you're shooting for, and sometimes it may feel like you're moving backward.

There's an old saying, "The dance of success is three steps forward, two steps back." Sometimes when you're experiencing the two steps back, it's hard to focus on solutions because you feel defeated. At times like this, just relax and remember you're simply dancing your way to success. Trust that as you work towards what you want instead of focusing on problems, ultimately you WILL get beautiful and amazing results!

Part 3: Multiple your Results

Here's another secret: your beautiful and amazing results compound as you consistently look for solutions and consistently "behave for the results you want." Note that I said "consistently," not "perfectly." You'll never be perfect. So, when you're not, shrug it off and start again. The more you work on creating results, the more your results grow! This is how you show up as the hero in your life.

In every great movie you watch, the hero faces challenges. Sometimes the hero even feels defeated. The movies that are the most fun to watch are movies where the hero is someone you relate to and want to be like. They are fun, smart, resourceful, a good friend, and clever. They always figure out a way to overcome their challenges, and often they inspire others to be better, too. This is how you multiply your results—by compounding your own amazing life and inspiring others to live amazing lives, too.

I'm excited to share with you the next steps in creating your life in the third book of this series. Until then, have fun showing up as the awesome and empowered *hero* that you are!

LIZ SEARS

About Liz Sears: Liz Sears lives her life in every way to fulfill her life mission which is to "inspire the masses to live lives full of connection, contribution, adventure, and impact." As a speaker and writer, she focuses on the consistency of striving towards becoming the best version of ourselves and sharing how to be awake and engaged in life. She fully believes that life, with its extensive variety of obstacles and opportunities, can be an amazing adventure. It's all about how we play the hand we were dealt and what we choose to create.

Liz has been married to her best friend since 1996 and together they have raised four wonderful sons. She is a proud alumna of Kent-Meridian High School and pursued Business Administration/Management at the University of Utah. Her roots trace back to Seattle Washington, but she and her family now call Layton, Utah home.

Beginning in the financial industry in 1995, Liz's career path has included roles such as Mortgage Loan officer, Property Manager, Real Estate Investor, and most recently as Team Leader and Associate Broker of Utah's Elite | REALTORS® at Real Brokers, LLC. She has served many times in leadership roles in the Real Estate industry including on the Board of Directors for the Northern Wasatch Association of Realtors and as a Governing Board Member of the Women's Council of Realtors Utah.

Author's Website: *www.LLLTWorldwide.com*

Book Series Website: *www.ThePrinciplesOfDebbieAndGoliath.com*

LORNA SHERLAND
FROM ME TO WE

Building Empowering Communities & Healing Trauma

I have lived much of my life in Lone Wolf territory: hunkering down, keeping myself to myself, figuring things out alone, and guarding against the pressures and judgments of the world.

I have also lived in a collaborative teamwork environment in corporate America: sharing space and holding space, letting myself be known by others, risking honesty, and figuring out how to make things work cohesively.

In the realm of empowerment, a profound journey exists from "me" to "we." This transition is not just a shift in perspective; it's a transformation of the self and the creation of supportive communities while still being grounded in one's own realized values and standards... Just like Debbie faced her Goliath, we too encounter challenges that shape our narratives, often leaving us feeling isolated or marginalized. Yet, within these struggles lie the seeds of empowerment and resilience.

I am the Debbie metaphor. Like many of you reading this book, I found myself navigating through life's adversities, carrying with me the weight of past experiences in silence. It was the tale of exclusion and marginalization from my high school groups. This narrative, though seemingly distant in time, had woven its tendrils deep into the fabric of my being, impacting my relationships, causing isolation, and inhibiting my ability to fully embrace community.

For years, I found myself trapped in the echoes of my past, feeling like an outsider even amidst social gatherings. My story continuously became a self-fulfilling prophecy, reinforcing the notion that I didn't belong. It wasn't until I confronted this narrative head-on that I realized its power over me. Then, through the work of transformation leadership training and continued personal development programs, the awareness of how deep this trauma was became evident as I did the work.

Acknowledging the impact of past trauma is the first step towards healing. Once you can recognize that the wounds from past years are still raw and that they demand attention as will be indicated in and by your mind and body, you will be on your way to inviting and attracting the support it will require to keep you on the road to the other side. If you understand that dwelling in victimhood perpetuates continuous pain, you can embark on a journey of self-discovery and healing. Embracing various modalities to support transformation is the preferred next step.

To show you how important the me-to-we theory is in the realm of healing, I want to share a recent story. I was attending a virtual webinar recently when a young lady raised her hand to share. First of all, let me set the stage. This event was a safe space created by the host to ensure that venerable shares would be honored. In her share, the young lady said that she did not have any traumas. Well, by the end of the event, she realized that she did have trauma—while not as graphic as someone being molested, she found the trauma that had been quietly operating in the background of her mind until she found this community.

While therapy is a great space and safe for transcending trauma, there is nothing like a safe community to hold space for discovery and transformation. Practicing mindfulness is another modality that can be learned to observe your thoughts and feelings without judgment, fostering a sense of inner peace and acceptance. Additionally, engaging in creative outlets such as writing, and art provided avenues for expression and catharsis.

It is important to realize that healing isn't a solitary endeavor. It required the nurturing embrace of community—a collective of individuals who uplifted and supported one another. This concept resonates deeply with the Blue Zone theory, which suggests that being super connected in a community enhances longevity and well-being and is intrinsically linked to strong social connections. It is said that Blue Zoners live well past 100 years old while still active and thriving and even participating in activities such as gardening and walking.

Blue Zones are regions around the world where people live significantly longer and healthier lives. What sets these communities apart is their emphasis on collective well-being and interdependence. In these tight-knit societies, individuals are not merely isolated entities but integral parts of a larger whole. They share meals, celebrate traditions, and support each other through life's ups and downs. There is one such group in Houston, Texas.

Drawing inspiration from the Blue Zone ethos, consider seeking to cultivate community—a tribe of like-minded individuals who shared your values of empowerment and growth. Together, you can embark on a journey of mutual support and collaboration, each contributing their unique strengths to the collective. Check out bluezoneproject.com

Creating such a community required vulnerability and courage. It meant opening up about past traumas and insecurities, knowing that they would be met with empathy and understanding. It meant stepping out of comfort zones and embracing discomfort as a catalyst for growth. Most importantly, it meant redefining the narrative from one of victimhood to one of empowerment.

In this supportive environment, you can find the courage to rewrite your story. Like me, I no longer see myself as the girl left out of high school cliques but now as a resilient woman who has overcome adversity and thrived despite it. My past has ceased to define me, and in its place emerged a newfound sense of purpose, belonging, and power!

The journey from "me" to "we" is not always easy, nor is it linear. It's a continuous process of self-discovery and community building, guided by the principles of empowerment and resilience. By confronting our past traumas and embracing supportive communities, we unlock the potential for healing and transformation. In doing so, we become the architects of our own empowerment, rewriting our stories and inspiring others to do the same.

This journey, however, is not without its challenges. Trauma, by its very nature, leaves a lasting imprint on our psyche, shaping our beliefs and behaviors in profound ways. Handling this trauma requires a multi-faceted approach—one that combines self-awareness, compassion, and resilience.

Mindfulness practices, such as meditation and yoga, offer additional support by cultivating present-moment awareness and fostering a sense of inner calm. By grounding ourselves in the here and now, we can gradually release the grip of past traumas and cultivate a deeper connection with ourselves and others.

Creative expression also plays a crucial role in trauma healing, allowing individuals to tap into their innate creativity and explore emotions that may be difficult to articulate verbally. Whether through writing, art, music, or dance, creative outlets provide a means of self-expression and catharsis, enabling individuals to transform their pain into something beautiful and meaningful. I started doing something as simple as puzzles to get my creative juices flowing. As I am writing this book, I see an idea where doing a puzzle even virtually can support the process as well.

Moreover, building supportive communities is essential for healing from trauma. Not that you have to air all of your business to everyone! Yet, by surrounding ourselves with caring and empathetic individuals, we create a safe space where our experiences are validated and our struggles are met with compassion. In these communities, we find strength in vulnerability and solidarity in shared experiences, empowering us to reclaim our narratives and rewrite our stories from a place of resilience and empowerment. How many girlfriends are in your inner circle?

It's important to acknowledge that healing from trauma is a journey that unfolds at its own pace. There will be setbacks and challenges along the way, but with patience, perseverance, and the support of a nurturing community, it is possible to move beyond the pain and reclaim our power.

The path to empowerment begins with embracing our past, cultivating self-compassion, and building connections that nourish the soul. In doing so, we not only heal ourselves but also create a ripple effect of healing and empowerment that extends far beyond our individual journeys and is so powerful. Together WE RISE!

This journey of healing and empowerment is not just about individual transformation; it's about creating a ripple effect of positive change that reverberates throughout our communities and beyond. As we heal our own wounds, we become beacons of hope and inspiration for others who may be walking a similar path. Our stories of resilience and triumph serve as a testament to the power of the human spirit and the possibility of transformation.

However, it's important to recognize that healing from trauma is not a linear process. There will be days when the pain feels overwhelming, when old wounds resurface with a vengeance. In these moments, it's crucial to lean on our support systems—to reach out to friends, family, or therapists who can provide comfort and guidance. It's also important to practice self-care and self-compassion, allowing ourselves the space to grieve, to feel, and to heal at our own pace.

Moreover, building supportive communities requires intentionality and effort. It means actively seeking out spaces where we feel seen, heard, and valued. It means being willing to be vulnerable and to show up authentically, even when it feels uncomfortable. And it means extending that same empathy and compassion to others, creating a culture of inclusivity and belonging where everyone feels welcome and accepted.

In the spirit of "we" let us come together as allies and advocates for each other's healing and empowerment. Let us lift each other up, celebrate each other's victories, and hold space for each other's struggles. And let us never underestimate the power of community to heal, to inspire, and to transform lives.

In conclusion, the journey from "me" to "we" is a profound one—one that requires courage, vulnerability, and resilience. It's a journey of self-discovery and community-building, guided by the principles of empowerment and healing. By confronting our past traumas, embracing supportive communities, and cultivating self-compassion, we unlock the potential for transformation and create a ripple effect of healing that extends far beyond ourselves.

Together, we have the power to rewrite our stories, reclaim our power, and create a world where everyone feels seen, heard, and valued and, in the words of Kathrine Woodward, "Call in the One," who is you, your true authentic self, thereby attracting your "we."

LORNA SHERLAND

About Lorna Sherland: Lorna Sherland is a distinguished Mindset Leadership Transformation Coach at Freedom LifeStyle, where she specializes in helping driven female entrepreneurs overcome limiting beliefs to achieve six- and seven-figure milestones in their businesses to create time and money freedom. Lorna combines her extensive experience in real estate with her passion for empowering others, focusing on educating buyers and sellers to enhance their real estate experiences while empowering female entrepreneurs to go to the net level of growth and impact.

As the founder of Success Power Brokers Real Estate and Consulting Services, with over 22 years of industry experience, Lorna has established herself as a Real Estate Mega Agent, successfully closing over 1,000 deals. Her philosophy is centered around the belief that a well-informed buyer or seller is the best consumer of her services. This dedication to client education has set a high standard in her field.

Lorna's journey in real estate began as a Broker in Newburgh, New York, where she committed to serving her clients far beyond their expectations, transferring her philosophy into practice. Additionally, she is a savvy Real Estate Investor, motivated by the goal of building wealth and creating a lasting legacy for her family, a principle she aligns with her biblical values.

Her academic background includes a bachelor's degree in finance, which has been instrumental in her successful career. Since August 2018, Lorna has dedicated herself to mindset empowerment and transformation coaching.

Lorna's impact extends beyond her professional achievements. She is a thought leader in the industry, frequently speaking on topics such as buyer and seller dynamics, real estate trends, mindset resets, and homeownership. Her insights and guidance continue to inspire and transform the lives of many, particularly female entrepreneurs aspiring to reach new heights in their business endeavors.

Author's Website: *www.LornaSherland.com*

Book Series Website: *www.ThePrinciplesOfDebbieAndGoliath.com*

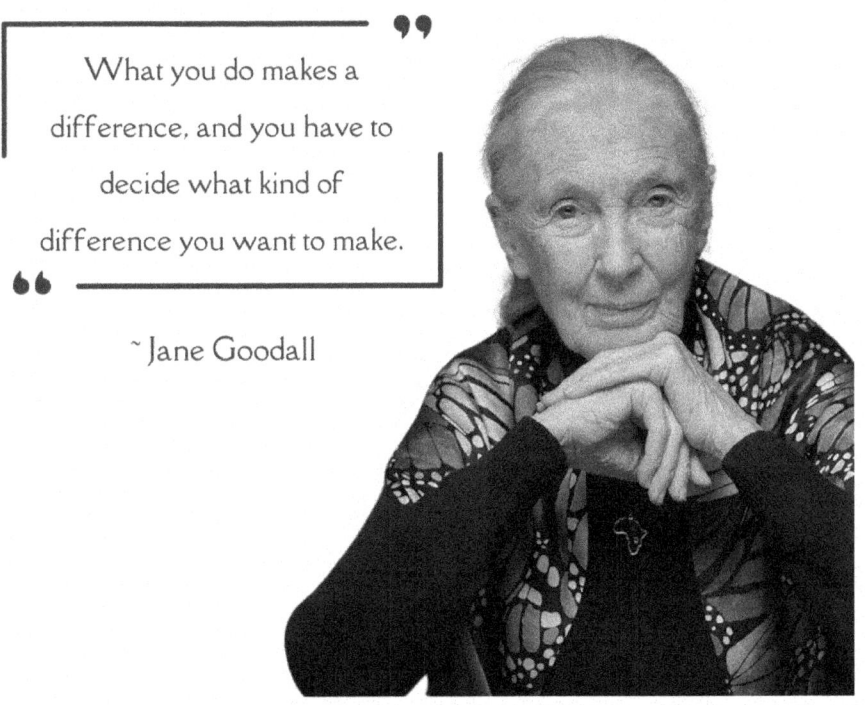

What you do makes a difference, and you have to decide what kind of difference you want to make.

~ Jane Goodall

M. A. FULTS
GIANT SLAYERS

Goliath was a giant of a man. *The Bible* (*Complete Jewish Bible* translation) tells us he stood nine feet nine inches tall. He wore a plate of armor weighing 120 pounds. The shaft of his spear was as big as a "weaver's beam" (2 to 2 1/2 inches in diameter) with an iron spearhead weighing fifteen pounds. One estimate has the entire spear weighing over 33 pounds. Which means Goliath was big, strong, and, according to The Bible, he had at least three brothers, possibly five, equally as big and strong. It is no wonder that David picked up five stones from the dry riverbed—he might have had to face more than one giant of a man that day. Yet, David was the one to step up.

In the chapter, "They Won't Get It Until You Do It" of his book *Mind Shift*, Erwin Raphael McManus writes about the importance of early man having someone be the first to eat a mushroom to see if it was good or poisonous: "Someone has to eat the mushrooms first, or else everyone will die of hunger. If no one goes first, there is no future. If no one goes first, we all die. The world is changed by the mushroom eaters. ... If you are playing it safe, you are playing to lose. The full measure of your gifts, and talents, and potential, and life, cannot be actualized if you are not willing to step into risk." When I read that, I realized, I have been and am a risk-taker. And every Giant-Slayer before me has been a risk-taker. And yet, none of us "Giant-Slayers" did so alone.

Every account of David facing Goliath shows him all by himself, with just his staff, shepherd's pouch, a sling and five stones. Yet the entire Israelite Army was standing, albeit with shaking knees, behind him. And, by his own account, "And David said, 'The Lord who saved me from the paw of the lion and the paw of the bear, He will save me from the hand of this Philistine." So Saul said to David, "Go, and may the Lord be with you'" (1 Samuel 17:37 New International Version). David had the Lord God of Israel and an army of men with him. But it was David who stepped out, faced down, and slew the giant. He was the One, the risk taker.

But there would have been no David, if David's great grandmother Ruth had not chosen to step up and take a risk. Ruth stepped forward numerous times. Once, when refusing to leave her mother-in-law Naomi, in order to stay in Ruth's home country, with her own people, as her sister-in-law chose. Once, when she swore covenant (verbal contract) with Naomi to stay with her, travel to Naomi's home country, and even to embrace Naomi's belief in One God, she proclaimed, "Your God will be my God!" And again, when she presented herself to Boaz, a potential "kinsman-redeemer," a man who could redeem Ruth and Naomi back into a family, a tribe, a nation.

The Bible tells us Ruth wasn't alone, either. Yes, she had Naomi, but she also had Naomi's God Whom she'd chosen to be her God. And Ruth had the townspeople of Bethlehem; they were joy-filled for Naomi's return, and welcoming to her daughter-in-law. She also had a man who was willing to protect her, and marry her. But first Ruth had to step up, to risk her reputation and even her life. First she had to eat the mushroom.

Stepping up, taking a risk, is never easy. Whether it is being the only woman in a class of male officers studying to become a Surface Warfare Officer on a ship, or being the first female Officer in Charge, and only Navy officer, onboard a USNS auxiliary ship—it's not easy. Through 20 years as a US Navy Officer, followed by 19 years as a Civilian Civil Servant, again working for the Navy, I was a risk taker, and very often was the first to step forward. I regret none of it. I am honored to have served, both in and for the Navy, and I know what I did, the risks and stepping forward as the one, forged a path for many, many women who have followed me.

I'm often asked two questions regarding my service; "Why did I chose to serve in the Navy?" and, "What was the best thing about your time serving?" Both have easy answers. I chose the Navy because I had, and still have, a romantic idea of going out to sea. To me, there is nothing better than being on the deck of a ship, any ship, with the wind in my face and the water rushing by the hull. Nothing better than looking up at a night sky with millions of stars visible because there are no city lights to interfere.

There is nothing better than rising for the early watch, coming up to a darkened bridge, and watching the Eastern sun rise over an empty ocean, slowly, yet inexorably rising up, crossing the sky, only to sink once again into the West, as I stand the evening watch. Oh, yes, there were people to manage and lead, paperwork to fill out and equipment to monitor, maintain and repair, but the time on watch was the most special time of all.

I loved, and still do, being underway, but on my first ship, USS AJAX (AR-6), where I was stationed onboard for 3 years, we only had a little over 8 months of underway time. Two and a third years were spent not underway, tied up to the pier. Which leads to my second love and the best thing about serving: The people, the men and women with whom I was privileged to serve. And while that is true for every duty station, ship or shore, on AJAX my relationship with the crew was very special. This is because of a choice I made before I reported aboard.

My commissioning source was Officer Candidate School (OCS) in Newport, RI. Most of the buildings had very long hallways (in Navy parlance "passageways"), and, with over 300 Officer Candidates, we would constantly be passing each other in the hall. Here's what I noticed: whenever two people passed each other they would say "hi," maybe "bye" and then move right on. No connection, no real interaction. This bothered me.

After leaving OCS, I determined that on my first ship, whenever I would meet someone in the passageway and they said "Hi" or "How are you?" I would stop, step in front of them, greet them by rank and name, and then engage them in a short, eye-to-eye-contact, conversation. There were over 650 officers and crew stationed on board AJAX during my three years, and by the time I transferred, I knew by sight and name at least 500 of them. And they knew me.

Was this stepping up? Risky? Well, yes, for me it was, because I'm an introvert, even more so forty years ago when this took place. Making myself known to so many, talking to them, being strong enough in my own sense of self to interrupt them, even though, at least initially, they hesitated to engage with me. That was risky, but oh so worth it. Who were the ones to stand with me, support me? It was the crew themselves. It was the men and women who banded together, with me, as a team when things became rough.

While I no longer remember most of them, every one that I've reconnected with over the intervening years has remembered me. This touches me to the core of my being. And my memories, even of the tough days, the days which lasted 24+ hours, the days of 3 hours sleep and double watches, those days were made better because of the relationships I established in my daily interactions of, "Hi, how are you, Petty Officer Smith? How is your daughter doing, and your study for the advancement exam?"

To my detriment, on my next ship I did not make the choice to engage others in the passageways. The predicable result was a tour not as enjoyable, and definitely not as rewarding. After analyzing the different experiences, I reverted back to my pushy, engaging self. Following tours were much better, with many life-long friendships the joyful outcome.

Of note: Those types of one-on-one engagements with resulting life-long relationships cannot come from social media. Eye-to-eye contact over Zoom will not provide the multiple inciteful cues about the other person, which are visible when standing face-to-face. There is no risk-taking when posting to a page or blog.

I'm still not an extrovert, but I no long allow my introverted self to stay in the corner of a room. I step up and take the risk that the other person might reject me...but that's on them, not me. Besides, they might find a new friend; better yet, a new life-long friend. So go out and meet someone today! Be a Giant-Slayer. Be the One to step up and eat the mushroom, slay the giant, forge the path. Because if you don't, someone else will, and you will miss out on a distinct blessing.

M. A. FULTS

About M. A. (MaryAlice) Fults: Born into an Army family, and with 39 years serving in and then working for the US Navy, means Fults spent many years traveling and living in foreign countries including four years in Teheran, Iran. She has a BFA in Drama Production from the University of AZ and a MS in Management from Naval Postgraduate School in Monterey, CA. After retiring for the second time in 2022, Fults continued her life-long pursuit of learning, while embarking on her new found passion of Heart Healing, Financial Advising and Life-Coaching. She has been blessed with one son.

Book Series Website: *www.ThePrinciplesOfDebbieAndGoliath.com*

MARIS SEGAL

LEADING WITH FOCUS & ALIGNMENT

Are you a leader? From a lens into your life at home, work and/or school, which of these actions do you engage in during a day or week: planning, directing, listening, sharing your goals and vision, guiding, running meetings, managing people and projects, delegating, scheduling, budgeting, organizing, influencing, negotiating, problem solving. While you may not have thought about yourself as a leader up until now, please hear yourself read these words, "I am the leader of my life." No one can change that. If you're a parent, you also lead a home team. And if you are an executive, supervisor, and/or entrepreneur, you also lead teams at work.

At any age and stage of life, personally or professionally, in every industry, accomplishments large and small are realized by being clear about what you want, creating a vision, building a plan, and seeing it through to reality with committed action. Ahh, if it were only that simple, right? Along the way, inevitable changes, often unexpected, will occur, caused by obstacles and distractions that will both test you and offer opportunities for resilience and growth.

In my Relational Leadership consulting and coaching work, we call these challenging times, "Goliath Moments & Goliath Opportunities." In these moments every individual leader has a choice: either succumb to the challenge or face it head on. Focus and Alignment support navigating through rough waters to stay on track with vision and change your relationship with the obstacles.

Focus from the Inside Out

Think of focus as a spotlight that illuminates your path, oftentimes amidst the darkness of uncertainty. Focus comes from a true commitment and attention to your vision and takes discipline to keep stepping forward with consistent action. Focus empowers you to concentrate your efforts and harness your strengths and resources effectively. Whether you're facing academic hurdles, personal challenges, or professional pitfalls, maintaining unwavering focus enables you to stay on track and make progress, step by step.

The results of focus can be positive or negative. That depends on your mindset. How you are feeling inside about yourself and the messages that are ringing in your head will impact how you are showing up in all of your relationships with family, friends, and colleagues. You may be familiar with the idea that "what you focus on grows." So, if you focus only on the problem when a Goliath moment occurs, it's likely that the problem will persist in some way or another. The alternative is to focus on creating a solution one action at a time so that you can rise as the victor versus becoming the victim to your circumstances.

From my earliest years, I was challenged in school as a slow reader, praying not to be called on and I never felt like I belonged. So, my value came from serving others and uniting humanity for the greater good. I loved meeting new people and connecting them with new experiences. When I saw opportunities to help others in any way, I was easily distracted which created some challenges!

I constantly heard my parents, teachers, tutors, and athletic coaches tell me to "focus." I often heard the statement from their frustration, so in my head I heard a demand—more like "FOCUS!" What I did not hear was "how to focus."

One day I was hanging out with my uncle who loved photography and we were looking through National Geographic magazines with photos of children impacted by war. When I saw these photos, my heart sank with sadness! In another issue, it featured images of tribal families—very different from the other publication. I felt such joy looking at their faces and daily lives. My uncle taught me that a photo is created first by seeing the big picture and then by seeing an image through a long lens which captures an important moment in time. He taught me how to focus on the image I want and how to adjust the lens to get more clarity. He went on to say that every image can spark a feeling.

This moment of clarity changed my life and focus became my friend. Committed to a future journalism career, I went on in my high school and college years to work on the yearbook and as a local newspaper reporter, radio announcer, and photographer.

A huge lesson from navigating the traumas and dramas of my youth was that when I was clear on what I wanted and intentional, committed to its completion, then facing Goliath moments head on seemed less daunting. I also learned that focus also builds confidence as each step towards our dreams gets to be a celebrated win.

Without focus, getting things done at all, let alone in excellence, is often time wasted on redirecting on a regular basis. Focus accompanied by alignment creates magical possibilities and impact. While focus provides clarity and direction to follow a plan and navigate through complexities, alignment ensures that your efforts are guided by authenticity and purpose. Together, they form a powerful synergy that enables individuals to confront challenges with resilience, determination, and a holistic approach that integrates both rational and emotional; in other words, our heads and hearts.

T.E.A.M. Alignment

Alignment begins with what you are committed to and knowing what is possible in your gut. That's your heart at work. Leading with your heart means tuning into your thoughts, aspirations, and intentions first, then gaining alignment with others. Engaging them in your vision and the feeling of completion can be inspiring. Your head plays an active role in strategizing, planning, and the actions you take to achieve what you are focusing on. In partnership, the head and heart create a powerful synergy that propels you towards realizing your vision.

This alignment serves as your guiding compass that keeps you and your team (at home and work) grounded and moving in the right direction, even when the journey gets tough and Goliaths pop up.

I'm often asked in my work if alignment and agreement are the same. The answer is no. That said, both have their place! Agreement is a finite decision by all involved to say, "I'm fully on board with this decision." Alignment leaves room for individual compromise where a few may not fully agree to the approach, yet they are still in support of the purpose and goal. Alignment is more crucial than agreement. Without it, nothing moves forward.

Alignment does not leave room for ego. I've learned to value the power of self-reflection and introspection from a place of discovery and curiosity versus judgment. Along the way, it's important to connect and evaluate to adjust to any shifts that have or may need to occur. Take the time to examine your own strengths, weaknesses, and motivations. Identify any limiting beliefs or self-imposed barriers that may be holding you back, and work towards overcoming them with determination and resilience.

Alignment offers great opportunities to collaborate and develop empowered relationships that will help bring your vision to life. Imagine a T.E.A.M. of skilled individuals working towards a shared objective. Tactically Enrolling Acute Minds – T.E.A.M. entails surrounding yourself with individuals who possess some of the skills that you may not. Each member brings their unique talents and perspectives to the table. It's their alignment towards a common mission that empowers them to collaborate and achieve together. From strategic thinkers to tactical workers, these are the people who not only offer valuable insights and perspectives but also challenge you to elevate your game and think outside the box.

Remember, you don't have to go it alone—collaboration and collective wisdom are powerful catalysts for overcoming obstacles and achieving your goals. When facing obstacles, tactically enrolling acute minds becomes invaluable. Seek out mentors, peers, or advisors who can provide guidance and support, drawing from their experiences and expertise to help you navigate through the toughest of challenges.

Be mindful of the company you keep. Surround yourself with individuals who uplift and inspire you, rather than those who drain your energy or detract from your focus. Cultivate a network of allies who share your values and aspirations, fostering an environment of mutual encouragement and growth.

Remember, Goliath will always make an attempt! Setbacks and failures are not signs of weakness, they are opportunities for growth and learning. Embrace them as valuable lessons that will ultimately strengthen your resolve and character. And always maintain faith in yourself and your abilities, knowing that with focus, alignment, and the support of tactically enrolled acute minds, you have the power to overcome any obstacle that stands in your way.

Imagine a world where we are all aligned and focused on evolving and elevating all of our relationships with ourselves and each other.

MARIS SEGAL

About Maris Segal: Maris Segal coaches, consults, and collaborates with executives, entrepreneurs, celebrities, and rising leaders to identify and bring their professional, personal, and philanthropic vision to life. Maris' focus on evolving human relation skills leverages her relationship marketing and mindset expertise with the power of "head and heart leadership" to build a peak performing culture of connected, confident individuals and teams for maximum impact. Often referred to as "America's Master Connectors," working alongside her husband Maris and Ken live by the philosophy that "We are all connected as human's first and that's where the bottom line begins." As authors, their book, *The RFactor*, a story of evolving relationships sits at the core of their work. In addition, Ken and Maris are sought-after speakers on stages, live events, and podcasts. They have been TEDx speakers and featured authors in 15 business and leadership-centered books.

Over four decades across thirty countries, she has served a wide spectrum of local and global leaders, brands, and policy makers. From board rooms and classrooms to Harvard, Super Bowl Halftimes and Papal events, Ken and Maris are also award-winning event producers known for uniting diverse populations with innovative cross-cultural marketing and personal development programs that bring a creative voice to issues, causes and brands. As certified Executive and Relationship coaches, they set a path for every client to build high performing businesses and elevate personal and professional leadership for maximum impact and a 360-degree thriving life! For a free RFactor Gratitude Practice Guide visit *www.SegalLeadershipGlobal.com*. Connect with Maris - *Info@SegalLeadershipGlobal.com*

Author's Website: *www.SegalLeadershipGlobal.com*

Book Series Website: *www.ThePrinciplesOfDebbieAndGoliath.com*

MEL MASON

THE MAGIC OF FOCUS & ALIGNMENT

Hello, dreamers! Today, I want to share with you the magical power of focus and alignment. These might sound like big words, but they are very important tools that can help you achieve your dreams and make the world a better place. Imagine you are an archer, and your goals are the targets. Focus and alignment are like the bow and arrow that will help you hit those targets with precision and joy. Let's dive into this adventure together and explore how you can use focus and alignment to shine brightly in everything you do.

Let's start with focus. Focus is the ability to concentrate on one thing at a time. Imagine you are reading your favorite book. If you are truly focused, you are so absorbed in the story that you forget everything else around you. That's what focus feels like. It's like having a superpower that lets you put all your energy into one task, making it easier to do your best.

Focus is important for achieving goals. When you focus on your goals, whether it's learning to play the piano, excelling in school, or becoming a great soccer player, you make steady progress. Each small step forward is a victory that brings you closer to your dreams.

When you are able to focus, you improve your skills. Practice makes perfect, but focused practice makes you a star. By concentrating on improving your skills, you can become very good at what you love to do. It's like watering a plant—with attention and care, it grows strong and beautiful.

Sometimes, too many thoughts can make you feel overwhelmed. Focusing on one thing at a time can help you feel calmer and more in control, like tidying up a messy room one toy at a time.

So, how do you improve your focus?

Setting clear goals is one way. Decide what you want to achieve and break it down into smaller steps. This makes it easier to focus on one task at a time.

Create a quiet space where you can concentrate without distractions. This could be a corner of your room, a spot in the library, or a cozy nook in your backyard. Carve out a space that you'll keep going back to in order to improve your focus.

Remember to take short breaks to rest your mind. After focusing for a while, a little break can help you come back refreshed and ready to continue. Resting is as important, if not more important than action.

Keep your study area neat and your schedule organized. Staying organized helps your mind stay clear and focused.

Mindfulness means paying attention to the present moment. When you practice mindfulness, you focus on what you are doing right now, rather than worrying about the past or the future. Practicing mindfulness helps you stay calm and focused.

Doing many things at once can make it hard to do any of them well. Avoid multitasking when you can and try to focus on one task at a time, giving it your full attention. This will help you complete it more efficiently and with better results.

Now let's talk about alignment. What is alignment? Alignment means making sure your actions, thoughts, and feelings are all pointing in the same direction. It's like making sure all the parts of a bicycle are working together so you can ride smoothly. When you are aligned, you feel balanced and true to yourself.

Why is alignment important? When you are aligned, you live authentically. You are true to yourself. You make choices that reflect who you are and what you believe in, which leads to a happier and more fulfilling life.

Alignment helps you feel confident because you know you are doing what is right for you. When you feel confident, that builds your confidence even more and this self-assurance makes it easier to face challenges and overcome obstacles.

Just like a well-tuned orchestra creates beautiful music, alignment brings harmony to your life. It helps you balance different aspects of your life, such as school, hobbies, and friendships.

Alignment isn't something that you get once and then stay aligned forever. It requires your attention and effort to stay aligned.

So, how can you stay aligned? By knowing your values. When you know your values, it helps you make decisions that align with who you are. It also makes it easier to say no to things that aren't in alignment. What's important to you? Is it kindness, honesty, creativity, or friendship?

Be sure to listen to your heart, your intuition. Pay attention to how you feel. If something doesn't feel right, it's okay to say no. Trust your instincts and make choices that make you happy and comfortable.

Know what works for you and what doesn't and learn to set boundaries to protect your time and energy. It's okay to say no to things that don't align with your goals and values.

Debrief daily. Take time to think about your actions and whether they reflect your true self. Journaling can be a great way to reflect and stay aligned with your inner values.

Surround yourself with positive influences. Spend time with people who support your goals and values. Friends and family who encourage you to be your best self can help you stay aligned and focused on what matters most.

Now what happens when you bring the two together—focus and alignment? When focus and alignment come together, they create a powerful force that helps you achieve your dreams and live a joyful life. Here are some ways to make them work for you:

Set Goals that Align with Your Values

Choose goals that reflect what is important to you. When your goals are aligned with your values, it's easier to stay focused and motivated.

Create a Vision Board

A vision board is a collection of images and words that represent your dreams and goals. It helps you stay focused on what you want to achieve and ensures your goals align with your values.

Practice Mindfulness

Mindfulness means being present in the moment and paying attention to your thoughts and feelings. It helps you stay focused and aligned by making you aware of what truly matters to you.

Celebrate Small Wins

Celebrate every small step you take towards your goals. This keeps you motivated and reminds you that you are on the right path.

Stay Flexible

Sometimes things don't go as planned, and that's okay. Being flexible and adapting to changes while staying focused on your goals and aligned with your values will help you navigate challenges and keep moving forward.

Focus and alignment are like the stars that guide your journey. They help you stay true to yourself and reach for your dreams with confidence and joy. Remember, you have the power to create a beautiful and meaningful life by staying focused on what matters and aligning your actions with your values.

Believe in yourself, trust your instincts, and let your light shine brightly. The world is waiting for your magic! Embrace the journey, cherish each step, and always remember that you are capable of achieving wonderful things. The sky is the limit, and with focus and alignment, you can reach for the stars.

MEL MASON

About Mel Mason: International, best-selling author, Mel Mason is The Clutter Expert, and as a sexual abuse survivor, she grew up depressed, suicidal, and surrounded by clutter. What she realized after coming back from the brink of despair and getting through her own chaos was that the outside is just a mirror of the inside. And if you only address the outside, the clutter keeps coming back. That set her on a mission to empower people around the world to get free from clutter inside & out, so they can experience happiness and abundance in every area of their lives.

Author's Website: *www.DeclutteringSpaces.com*

Book Series Website: *www.ThePrinciplesofDebbieAndGoliath.com*

DR. ONIKA SHIRLEY

THE POWER OF UNITY

"Unity is strength. When there is teamwork and collaboration, wonderful things can be achieved"
~ **Mattie Stepanek**

In the depths of every individual resides a burning passion, a fervor that ignites a desire to impact the world positively, to uplift others, and to foster meaningful change. This inner flame, fueled by a profound love for humanity and a steadfast belief in the strength of unity, has always guided me on my journey.

The wise words of Mattie Stepanek reverberate within me as I set forth on this path: "Unity is strength. When there is teamwork and collaboration, wonderful things can be achieved." These words hold great significance for me, as I have personally witnessed the profound transformations that occur when individuals unite, driven by a common purpose and shared vision.

I have been privileged to see the beauty of people coming together in harmony, supporting one another, and standing resilient in the face of challenges. It is this spirit of togetherness, this unyielding faith in the collective power of humanity, that propels me to inspire, empower, and ignite change in the hearts of those around me. As I embark on this new chapter, I am reminded of the boundless potential that emerges when we unite, when we set aside our differences and stand as one. This unity is a beacon of hope, a guiding light that shines through the darkness, illuminating the path toward a brighter, more cohesive future.

Throughout my journey as a woman working in manufacturing, I have encountered numerous challenges and setbacks in a predominantly male-dominated environment. Yet, I have always approached these obstacles with unwavering determination, resilience, and a commitment to continuous growth. My experiences in manufacturing have not only refined my skills and expertise but have also allowed me to extend a helping hand to others, especially women, who aspire to excel in any field they choose.

In sharing my journey, I hope to create a space where readers can see themselves reflected in my experiences and realize that they have the power and potential to overcome challenges and thrive in any endeavor they set their sights on. By embracing a collaborative and collective approach, we can support and uplift one another, fostering a community where mentorship, advocacy, and solidarity form the foundation for growth, resilience, and success in any field. Together, we can create a network that empowers each individual to reach their full potential and achieve their aspirations, no matter the path they choose to pursue.

By embracing the power of resilience and determination, we can inspire each other to push past limitations and strive for greatness in every aspect of our lives. It is through our shared experiences and supportive network that we can uplift one another, providing guidance and encouragement along the way.

I believe that every woman has the potential to excel in whatever endeavor she chooses, and it is my mission to help cultivate that belief in others. By fostering a culture of empowerment and support, we can create a world where women are encouraged to pursue their passions, break barriers, and shatter stereotypes.

Together, let us continue to uplift, inspire, and empower one another on this journey towards success and fulfillment. No dream is too big, and no goal is out of reach when we stand united in our pursuit of excellence. Let us embrace our strength, resilience, and unwavering determination as we forge ahead, paving the way for a brighter and more inclusive future for all.

We Foundation

As we continue this journey of empowerment and growth, I want to share 5 key actions that we can take to not only cultivate our own success but also serve as a steppingstone for others:

1. Mentorship: Offer guidance, support, and mentorship to those who may be navigating similar challenges or seeking to advance in their careers. Sharing your experiences and insights can provide invaluable support and inspiration to others on their journey.

2. Advocacy: Advocate for gender equality, diversity, and inclusion in all aspects of life. By speaking up and taking action, we can help create a more equitable and supportive environment for women in all fields and industries.

3. Networking: Build and nurture a strong network of like-minded individuals who share your values and goals. Collaborating with others can open new opportunities, foster growth, and create a sense of community and support.

4. Continuous Learning: Embrace a mindset of continuous learning and growth, seeking out opportunities for personal and professional development. By investing in your own skills and knowledge, you can better position yourself to succeed and inspire others to do the same.

5. Paying It Forward: As you achieve your own goals and milestones, remember to pay it forward by supporting and uplifting others along the way. Whether through mentorship, advocacy, or simply lending a listening ear, your actions can have a ripple effect, creating a more supportive and inclusive world for all.

By taking these actions to heart and incorporating them into our daily lives, we can not only empower ourselves but also serve as a beacon of inspiration and support for those around us. Together, we can create a community where women are encouraged to excel, thrive, and make a lasting impact in any endeavor they choose to pursue.

Embrace Your Inner Strength

In the tapestry of life, each of us holds a thread of infinite potential and power. Yet, for some, the journey towards self-belief and empowerment may seem daunting, obscured by doubt and fear. To the woman who has not yet realized her own strength and potential, I offer these words of encouragement and inspiration.

You can achieve greatness beyond your wildest dreams. Within you lies a reservoir of untapped strength, resilience, and courage waiting to be unleashed. It is time to shed the cloak of self-doubt and embrace the truth of your own worth and capabilities.

As you navigate the pages of empowerment and inspiration, let the stories of resilience, determination, and triumph ignite a spark within you. Allow yourself to be inspired by the women who have walked before you, who have faced adversity with unwavering resolve and emerged stronger and more empowered than ever.

Today, I challenge you to take the first step towards your own empowerment journey. Believe in yourself and your abilities. Take a leap of faith and trust in the power that resides within you. Embrace your uniqueness, your voice, and your dreams with unwavering conviction. Do not be afraid to seek support and guidance from those around you. Surround yourself with a tribe of like-minded individuals who uplift and inspire you. Together, you can create a community of empowerment and encouragement, where each woman is celebrated for her unique gifts and contributions.

Remember, the path to empowerment is not always easy, but it is always worth it. Embrace the challenges, the setbacks, and the moments of doubt as opportunities for growth and self-discovery. With each obstacle you overcome, you become stronger, more resilient, and more empowered than ever before.

So, dear woman, I urge you to take action. Step into your power, your strength, and your worth. Embrace the journey of self-discovery and empowerment with courage and determination. You are capable of achieving greatness, of inspiring others, and of making a lasting impact on the world around you. Believe in yourself, take that first step, and watch as the world opens up before you, full of endless possibilities and opportunities. Your time is now. Embrace your inner strength and let your light shine brightly for all to see.

In conclusion, in the intricate weaving of life, each woman holds the power to create a masterpiece of strength, resilience, and empowerment. As we journey through the chapters of self-discovery and inspiration, may we remember that our potential knows no bounds. Let us embrace our uniqueness, our voices, and our dreams with unwavering conviction.

Together, we can create a tapestry of empowerment and inspiration, where each thread contributes to a vibrant and diverse tapestry of strength and unity. Let us continue to support and uplift one another on this journey towards empowerment, knowing that our collective power is unstoppable. As we stand together, united in purpose and determination, we can create a world where every woman believes in her own worth and capabilities. The time for action is now. Let us step boldly into our power and shine brightly, illuminating the path for generations of women to come.

Strength is not measured by the battles we avoid, but by the courage we show in facing them head-on. It's time to face your Goliath.

DR. ONIKA SHIRLEY

About Dr. Onika L. Shirley: Dr. Onika L. Shirley is the Founder and CEO of Action Speaks Volume, Inc. She is a Procrastination Strategist and Behavior Change Expert and known for building unshakable confidence, stopping procrastination, and getting your dreams out of your head into your life. She is a Master Storyteller, International Speaker, Serves in Global Ministry, International Best-Selling Author, International Award Recipient, Serial Entrepreneur, and Global Philanthropist impacting lives in the USA, Africa, India, and Pakistan.

Dr. O is a Motivational Speaker and Christian Counselor. Dr. Onika is the Founder and Director of Action Speaks Volume Orphanage Home and Sewing School in Telangana State, India, Founder and Director of Action Speaks Volume sewing school in Khanewal and Shankot, Pakistan. She founded, operated, and visited an Orphanage home in Tuni, India for four years and she supported widows in Tuni, India. She is the founder of Empowering Eight Inner Circle, ASV C.A.R.E.S, ASV Next Level Living Program, and P6 Solutions and Consulting. She has served for 13 years as a therapeutic foster parent for the State of. Of all the things Dr. O does she is most proud of her profound faith in Christ and her opportunity to serve the body of Christ globally.

Author's Website: *www.ActionSpeaksVolumes.com*

Book Series Website: *www.ThePrinciplesOfDebbieAndGoliath.com*

One child, one teacher, one book, one pen can change the world.

~ Malala Yousafzai

RACHEL CORPUS
WHO YOU TRULY ARE

In the early 1980's, my parents, my older brother, and I were hit by a drunk driver on our way back from a movie. I was four.

Little did I know I was about to have a near-death experience that would alter my life.

Mom and Dad had this giant green car. I loved it. There was enough room for me to fit in between Mom and Dad in the front seat on top of the center console. I felt like the queen of the road! Hey—it was the 80's. Rules were different then.

I was asleep when the other car hit us. I woke up to the taste of blood and starburst. I remember the sound of screeching and then silence. The impact of the accident forced me down on my mom's feet. I was in a ball, holding myself tightly.

The smell of flowers filled the car—I mean REALLY filled the car. "How strange," I remember thinking. And then the music started. It was loud, and I just thought it was from the radio. But I knew about this music. It sounded like the music my dad played on his record player—it was classical, stringed music. But as I thought that thought, the music began to change in a way that is hard for me to explain. I didn't just hear it; I began to feel it. It was around me, and in me. Like it was a part of me.

The next thing I remember, I was no longer in the car. And I was not alone. There was someone behind me. She didn't talk to me out loud, but she communicated. Just as I was about to ask a question, her answer was in my mind. It's like this being knew my thoughts at the same time I did. And the amount of love I felt was like none I had ever felt before.

You might be wondering how I remember this so vividly. It happened when I was four, after all. Well, when I left my body, I was no longer four years old. I was older. Or, rather, I was no age. I was talking in my usual Rachel voice, but no longer as a child. I was Rachel. I had returned to myself as a soul.

This is why I can remember my NDE. This isn't the same as a memory from my childhood. I am not remembering through the lens of a four-year-old. I am remembering something from my fully developed soul's mind that happened 43 years ago. The details remain fresh in my mind still today.

The Angel continued to speak: "Try your wings. You still have them."

I felt a burning sensation between my shoulder blades where one might think Angel wings attach. As I felt this, I felt my essence begin to move rapidly. I could see her now, and I knew we had always been connected. As we moved together, she told me the following:

"Rachel, you, too, are an Angel of God and you are from this Angelic Realm. You were given a sacred mission to guide earth into the thousand years of peace within your lifetime. There are more of you on earth. Some will know they are like you, some will not. Religion will not support you, so you must surrender yourself to spirituality. All things are created by God. Do all things within the Light of God, and your mission cannot fail. There will be seasons when you do not remember your value. When the time is right, you will remember your Angelic origin once again."

The Angel showed me how badly I had been hurt in the accident. My brain had endured severe damage that would not effectively be caught by the doctors until much later in life. The three brain fractures that were immediately visible would be one thing, but the long-term trauma would cause learning issues, memory loss, seizures, headaches, and depression.

But my family would be so sad. I saw that if I stayed behind, my mission would go on. I was special, but I was also one of many. But I said yes to something, and that was important. I did not understand the importance of my little piece of the Universal puzzle, but if it was going to be important enough for me to have a meeting like this, in God's stomping grounds, I was going to fulfill that promise.

The Angel told me one last thing. My Spirit was big. Literally BIG. If I decided to go back, God was going to squish me back into my little body, and it was going to hurt. So, on the count of three, think of the happiest thing I could think of. And so, I did…

The next thing I saw was my dad, all bandaged up, doing his Grover impression from Sesame Street! I laughed and then squinted from the pain. Ouch! My head hurt and my body felt so tiny compared to the vastness it just was a moment ago.

Over time, my NDE began to fade. I didn't forget it; I just went into the background so I could be a kid again. And, honestly, this story is hard for a lot of people to believe. The fading back of my NDE forced me to build a partnership with God that is collaborative. It became clear to me that this Angel in a human body business did not mean life was going to be easy. Oh, no—quite the opposite. And so, I began to integrate my trauma with balance. I managed the mystical and the practical. I had to: I was seeing Spirit…Angels were now communicating with me. I was seeing the dead. I could understand animals. My world was changing.

My Angels began to appear through everyday people: teachers, mentors, peers, students, favorite authors. And I made a choice to listen and gobble up every bit of wisdom they had to share with me. Where there was an obstacle, I saw it as an invitation to ask for more.

I began to look at this world through two lenses: a human lens and an angelic lens. For many years, I led a very mainstream life. I was a schoolteacher, then a religious education teacher, and then I even attended seminary and became a minister. But there was always a cry in my heart to go deeper. And so I did. I embraced my mainstream lens, and I added a lens of wonder. Through daily meditation, self-evaluation, and study of ancient texts from other religions and belief systems besides my own, I began to remember who I came here to be: to live my Truth as an Angel in human form.

What is an Angel, anyway? I am a messenger. What message do I have to share with you, reading this story today? I want you to know that when you align with who you are—who you really are—your life will respond back to you in a positive way.

Focus in on your definition of success, so you can draw it to you. And then, create a process you can align with each day. For me, it was a balance between the mystical and the practical. What is it for you? Once you create the process that is truly yours, it will become your oxygen. Bend the parameters of your matrix—because it is yours to create with Source! Spread YOUR wings, Dear One! It's time.

RACHEL CORPUS

About Rachel Corpus: Rachel Corpus is a psychic medium and Angel communicator who specializes in helping people connect with their highest purpose and connect to the Source of God Energy. Rachel connects with people on the other side, Angels, animals, Light beings, Starseeds, and a very special collective of extraterrestrials who call themselves SARAI. Rachel specializes in connecting through the quantum realm, the multiverse, parallel dimensions, and past/other lifetimes. You may find Rachel working with people on television, radio, large audiences, on her podcast, or working one-on-one with clients. Learn more by visiting Rachelcorpus.com.

Author's Website: *www.RachelCorpus.com*

Book Series Website: *www.ThePrinciplesOfDebbieAndGoliath.com*

SALLY WURR

ADAPT, ACHIEVE, THRIVE

"Stay committed to your decisions but stay flexible in your approach. It's the end you're after."
~ **Anthony Robbins**

In this journey called life, we encounter various challenges, setbacks, and uncertainties that test our strength and determination. The ability to navigate these obstacles with grace and bounce back from adversity is known as inner resilience. This quality plays a pivotal role in shaping our character, fostering personal growth, and ultimately leading us towards a more fulfilling and empowered existence.

By embracing challenges, it empowers you to view them as opportunities for growth rather than insurmountable barriers. It reminds you that you can face any Goliath that comes your way and emerge stronger on the other side.

You develop new skills, expand your perspective, and build confidence in your abilities the more times you face it head on. Your ability to adapt to change is crucial for personal growth. Resilience allows you to navigate transitions and uncertainties with flexibility and grace, fostering a sense of balance for life.

Setbacks are inevitable in life and the sooner you learn to overcome them, the better. Navigating through life's hurdles and enhancing inner resilience demands a comprehensive strategy, open communication, self-reflection, and reaching out to reliable sources of support. Engaging in conversations with parents or mentors enables you to acquire crucial advice, support, and motivation, making a journey through challenges with resilience and fortitude. Approaching obstacles with honesty and openness can significantly bolster inner strength, personal development, and a resilient outlook.

Leverage the strength of open communication to tackle challenges fearlessly.

Many young people face challenges, like peer pressure and the struggle to meet group expectations. The fear of being judged or criticized by others can suppress uniqueness, creativity, and personal development. Developing your critical thinking is crucial to enhancing your ability to question assumptions, seek evidence, and contemplate different viewpoints.

I encourage you to broaden your horizons by engaging in reading, discussions, and immersing yourself in varied cultures and experiences. Overcoming hurdles like peer pressure and fear of judgment is vital for young individuals to appreciate diverse viewpoints and build resilience.

In order to cultivate your critical thinking skills, I recommend a three-step approach:

1. Cultivate curiosity and skepticism: I encourage you to question the world around you and challenge assumptions that seem incorrect or feel off. This will foster a more curious and analytical mindset, crucial for long term personal and professional growth.

2. Evaluate information critically: Learn how to critically assess the reliability of your information sources. I would encourage you to confirm the accuracy of information before it shapes your opinions or decisions. Improving the ability to analyze received information, whether heard or read, is foundational for informed growth. It is always my recommendation that you look at several resources for proof.

3: Engage in problem solving: I would encourage you to participate in activities that require critical and creative thinking. This practice helps you learn to tackle challenges from various perspectives, enhancing your problem-solving skills and ability to think outside the box.

When it comes to fighting the Goliaths of the world, there are many different strategies you can learn to make it easier.

My own journey into mastering these skills began in 7th grade. My father was in the Air Force, which meant we moved around the United States often. By the time I entered 4th grade, we had lived in 8 states, pushing me well beyond my comfort zone from a young age. This lifestyle taught me the art of integrating with diverse groups through my involvement in numerous sports and activities. By 7th grade, my repertoire included tap dancing, baton twirling, baseball, softball, and bowling.

I quickly learned to "cultivate my curiosity" by engaging in many different activities. It also gave me quite a bit of exposure to challenging events that I needed to learn to navigate without having a melt-down.

We lived on Minot Air Force Base in North Dakota when I was in 4th grade. We stayed there until I finished 8th grade. In addition to the sports I involved myself in, I also became involved in our community youth center. Here, I undertook student leadership roles in organized activities for younger children. This early exposure to leadership not only insulated me from the impact of peer influence, but also equipped me with a personal road map for navigating adolescence.

Every Saturday morning, I was part of a bowling team, an experience that taught me the importance of teamwork and the value of accepting advice to improve my skills. Bowling is a sport that offers numerous valuable lessons. Bowling hones your hand-eye coordination, requiring precise aim and release of the ball to consistently hit targets and improve scores. It demands focus and concentration, pushing you to pay attention to your game for success.

My commitment to bowling was recognized when my parents bought me my own bowling ball and shoes, a significant turning point. Learning to adapt to how my bowling ball reacted under different lane conditions was a mix of practice and skill. Recognizing and adjusting to the lane conditions, such as freshly polished lanes or dealing with "tracking marks" left by previous bowlers, required strategic thinking and adaptability.

It was during this time that I learned to "evaluate information critically," as I had many people sharing their knowledge with me. I had to make the decision to accept their information or to reject it. This learning curve took me awhile to navigate. It was also a time that I learned how to "read" people's body language and their words. I learned to quickly decide whether they were a friend or foe. Many times, figuring out who you do not want to be around is more important than those you keep close.

Being a part of the bowling team emphasized the collective effort toward achieving the top spot in leagues and tournaments. It was about mutual support, sharing triumphs, and mastering the art of winning or losing with grace. This experience underscored the importance of maintaining composure during victories and defeats, a valuable early life lesson.

This was also where I learned to "engage in problem-solving" by listening and learning from the members of my team and our coach.

The final skill I would like to share is goal setting and perseverance. By setting your own personal goals for improvement and working hard to achieve them can teach you the importance of perseverance and dedication.

I was the youngest bowler on my team and the only female. I became a great bowler because of my teammates and the lessons in life and bowling skills they taught me. They treated me like a "favorite" little sister. Ultimately, they wanted to win, and they knew by making sure I was able to be my best helped their cause.

I remember in 8th grade, our team won our club championship. It qualified our team and each of us as individuals to compete at the regional tournament. We had to go to a city a couple of hours away for the tournament, which was also a learning experience. It was the first time I went somewhere without my parents. There were parent chaperones, but I was still responsible for handling my money and to be where I was supposed to be to compete on time.

Our team took first place at the regional tournament and each of us also won in our respective age categories. I bowled way above normal, which allowed me the top spot for my age. It was a very joyous and happy bus ride back home.

Cultivating having a good balance of both planning and flexibility in your approach to life makes it easier to manage your time and responsibilities effectively. It is important to have a road map to follow, but also be willing to adapt and make changes when necessary. Having mentors to turn to for guidance and support is a smart way to navigate through challenges and make informed decisions.

Remember, it is okay to ask for help and not put too much pressure on yourself. Keep up the good work in finding what works best for you! If you ever need assistance or advice, feel free to reach out.

"Enjoying success requires the ability to adapt. Only by being open to change will you have a true opportunity to get the most from your talent."
~ Nolan Ryan

SALLY WURR

About Sally Wurr: Sally Wurr is an international speaker and Multi-Best-Selling-Book Author.

Sally is known as the "Storm Whisperer" because her message is about how to prepare for life's storms. Each person has trials and tragedies, but it is how we react to those events that help us grow and survive in our business and personal activities.

By sharing her expertise with stories, she teaches you how to embrace change and how to face life's struggles head-on. Simply put, she likes to teach others how to problem solve.

Sally embraces the knowledge that those who can must be the ones that do. She shares her stories so that others can find their true purpose.

In addition to writing and speaking, Sally is the President and Founder of SW Insurance Corp. She has helped thousands of CEOs develop employee benefits programs to attain and retain employees. It is her problem-solving and attention to detail that have made her successful in this arena for many years.

Author's Website: *www.SallyWurr.com*

Book Series Website: *www.ThePrinciplesOfDebbieAndGoliath.com*

SARAH LEE

MY WHY FOR MONEY MENTOR®

The last conversation my parents ever had with each other was when I was nine years old. I realize I was fortunate to have them both for that long, but I want to remind you never to take your family and supporters for granted. You never know what your life would be like without them. I do.

When people see me, they're often shocked to find out that I grew up practically an orphan. This experience shaped me into the unique and brilliant Sarah Lee I am today.

Without a family, you get used to no one remembering your accomplishments, your birthday, or thanking you for your efforts. You must create all that yourself. As a Success and Mindset Expert, author, speaker, businesswoman, and philanthropist, I've found it most challenging to stay humble and human.

No one will cheer you on during the struggle to become impactful or successful. People who don't know your background might belittle your achievements because they see you as "superhuman." They're often more interested in their own stories than yours. Being a unicorn is hard—harder than just going along with the crowd and being invisible.

When I was nine, I became the translator between my parents and the real world. They divorced when I was five. My mother, a successful real estate agent, bought my dad a house a few blocks away from our family home to give my brother and me a semblance of normalcy. It was a huge sacrifice and one of the most unique and clever ideas for a divorce arrangement I've ever heard. I highly recommend it if you can do it.

Fast Forward the story, a few years later.

Unfortunately, my dad started dating one of my mom's friends, Joni. One night, he got caught dropping Joni off after a date. Joni's ex-husband, hiding in the bushes, attacked my dad as he sat trapped in the car with his seatbelt on.

Joni was someone I knew well. My dad used to house-sit for her and take us to her house. I didn't know they were dating until my dad ended up in the hospital after that beating. That was when I started to grow up.

My parents stopped talking to each other after that incident. The only other conversation they had was at my college graduation when I was the commencement speaker for the Art History Department at UCLA. I had been elected President of the Art History Association and worked at a new museum in Downtown LA, teaching people about the Chicano experience. I am not Chicano, but growing up in a close community, I had to translate a lot for my parents. When my mother and I left our community, we were abandoned by our family, labeled as traitors for leaving.

Chicanos are primarily first-generation Americans or those born in Mexico who now live in the U.S. They're not fully accepted as Americans or Mexicans, so they develop their own culture. My work with the Chicano community was a labor of love, influenced by my own experiences of displacement and forming my own identity.

But back to my parents not talking anymore.

My parents lived a few blocks apart, and my older brother, at eleven, wasn't interested in taking on the responsibility of communication for the family. So, I became the communicator. I was kind, thoughtful, and smart. I had already been on TV, hosting a PBS show and reading the news weekly. So, at nine, I took over the family communication—

arranging pickups, schedules, and who needed what. It was scary, but I learned to overcome fear through self-talk, meditation, and prayer.

My dad was so angry at my mom for being upset about Joni that he stopped talking to her. The only way our family could communicate was through me. That's how I learned the power of choice and maturity. I learned never to fight with people you love—you might never recover from it.

At nine, I handled all family responsibilities while working as a child TV personality and newscaster. My parents stopped focusing on me and started focusing on what I could do for them. Although the station still exists today, they kept no footage or pictures of my time there.

Growing up like this was challenging, but I handled it so naturally and with such grace that most people never knew what was happening. This experience led me to study developmental psychology and behavioral therapy at UCLA. I wanted to understand what a normal childhood looked like since I didn't have one.

This background fueled my passion for helping people without a voice. No one knows better than I do what it feels like to voice the voiceless, which is both a blessing and a curse. By the time I was in college, I had been teaching and talking professionally for over 15 years. This experience allowed me to teach Acting and Improv at UCLA while studying psychology, art, and art history.

Living in Los Angeles, I worked inside the UCLA Resnick Neuropsychiatric Hospital. Loyola Marymount's Graduate Program heard about my work with nonverbal children in the hospital and recruited me for art therapy. I was brilliant at it, understanding people in ways that others couldn't.

I can see who someone is by talking to them for just a few minutes. Behavior, tone, eye movements, and actions reveal their intentions and capabilities. After decades of practice, you get pretty good at understanding people if you want to survive.

Despite my academic success and professional achievements, I longed for recognition from someone I loved. My family couldn't give that to me because we had become strangers.

At 11, during a real estate slump, my mother married her boyfriend, who hated kids. He had abandoned his own three children and didn't want to be a full-time father. This was a recipe for disaster. After 12 months, he tried to punch me in the face. I ducked, and six months later, they separated. My mother was sad for years, working and coming home in despair.

At 15, my mother bought me a car to drive to school, which was an hour and a half away. I had a CIF championship boyfriend, and his family became my surrogate family for the next five years. I learned to serve others to get my emotional needs met.

Serving others is the easiest way to turn strangers into friends and meet your basic emotional needs. My father, a city councilman, taught me this through our civic work and his private detective work and insurance fraud investigations.

Now, you have to understand that since I was already working and the primary organizer for the family, I was able to absorb many of the lessons that you can learn from being a writer or a private investigator while you were still a child.

Growing up like this helped me understand how to communicate with nonverbal children. Loyola Marymount recruited me for art therapy, but I felt it was a trap. Revisiting my wound repeatedly was too much for my young mind to handle.

At the time, I felt like in order to make money and be successful, I had to revisit my wound over and over again, and when opportunities were presented to me, I remembered I was an orphan with zero family support and zero family awareness. I felt that that kind of work, while honorable, was way too much for my little mind to handle and focus on in a clinical setting on a daily basis.

So, I pursued modeling, acting, event planning, and fundraising for nonprofits, primarily art museums and collections. My gift was in psychology, but I traveled the world learning about art firsthand, self-funding my education. Emotionally, I ran.

My father, fearing travel, hasn't seen me more than ten times since I turned 18 unless I visited him. Despite his love for me, we remain strangers. Helping him get serious about his wife of 40 years, a world-famous Latin American Scholar, was his way of connecting with me.

I share this story not for sympathy but to explain why I am passionate about teaching financial literacy, mental health, performance, self-care, and goal setting. This is the foundation of Money Mentor®—a program I built to teach kids and adults financial literacy and money mindset. My expertise in these subjects stems from making critical decisions at nine years old.

SARAH LEE

About Sarah Lee, MBA: A brilliant educational psychologist and leadership expert by education, Sarah Lee is the innovative author of *"Rock Soup - An Innovational Idea in Leadership."* By profession, Sarah has been teaching financial literacy for the last 15 years using her own firm as a platform. She is a full-service financial advisor and manager of her own Securities Branch of a national firm. In addition, she networked with 100 Brokers all over the US. Sarah has an MBA in Finance and Social Impact and is 14 months shy of a Ph.D. in Educational Leadership. She is also the founder of multiple other companies and brands. She is now mostly currently focused on her production company with her husband, MONEY MENTOR, LLC™.

She has been advocating and speaking on large issues like financial literacy, literacy, mindset, clean water, and service to the world (hunger, water issues, poverty, and literacy) for her entire life. She is the child of a public servant. Her father was a writer (he wrote textbooks on risk and insurance practices), a city councilman in a small town who taught Sarah civic duties, service to the public, and how the national political system works. She learned how to serve others, run a nonprofit volunteer group, and make a community impact. That led to an opportunity to be "on TV (not streaming) weekly as a host" as a nine-year-old. The opportunity became more interesting when they asked Sarah what she would like to produce for Kids-4 TV. She said, "I would like to host a consumer reports show, where I would interview local business owners and see how I could highlight them while giving them ways to give back and make a difference." She was nine. That led to a life of public speaking, running endowments, and working with local universities on educational issues. She developed her world-famous business philosophy during this time: "Business is just like Rock Soup..."

Learn more about Sarah Lee, MBA, and follow her on FB: @coachmeSarahLee, @moneymentormethod; Instagram: @moneymentorcompany, @coachmeacademy. For Money Tips, you can text the words "MONEYMENTOR" to 55444 for a free gift or visit our webpage: linktr.ee/MoneyMentorMethod.

Author's Website: *www.MoneyMentorFreeGift.com*

Book Series Website: *www.ThePrinciplesOfDebbieAndGoliath.com*

STEPH SHINABERY

YOUR GENIUS MACHINE— FOCUS & ALIGNMENT AWAKENED

Embracing Your Unique Path

In the first volume of The Principles of Debbie and Goliath, I shared my journey of finding my voice and strength through the battles I faced growing up and navigating adulthood. From towering over my peers to breaking barriers in sports, each challenge taught me valuable lessons in resilience and determination. In this chapter, I aim to delve deeper into the art of focus and alignment, building on those foundational principles to empower you in your journey toward personal and professional fulfillment.

The Power of Alignment

Alignment is not just a buzzword; it's a powerful state of being where your actions, goals, and values are in harmony. It's about living a life that is true to who you are, allowing your inner compass to guide you. This concept became clearer to me as I navigated my career and personal growth. Initially, I followed a path dictated by societal expectations and external pressures. I chose nursing from a place of 'shoulds'—I should have a stable job, I should pursue a reliable career. However, these choices, while practical, left a void that couldn't be filled by mere accomplishments or financial stability.

I discovered that true alignment comes from recognizing and embracing your unique strengths and passions. For me, it was the creative expression I found in art and the fulfillment of helping others awaken to their potential through coaching. This realization was the catalyst for developing the Genius Identity Code™, a process to unlock your gift, purpose, and path.

Your Gift: The Cornerstone of Focus

Understanding your gift is the first step towards achieving alignment. Your gift is that innate talent or ability that comes naturally to you. It's the thing you do so effortlessly that you might not even recognize it as special. Reflecting on my journey, I realized that my gift lies in creative problem-solving and inspiring others to see and believe in their potential.

To identify your gift, consider the activities that energize you, the skills that others frequently seek your help with, and the tasks you find yourself gravitating towards even without external incentives. Your gift is the foundation upon which you can build a life of purpose and fulfillment.

Purpose: The Fuel for Your Journey

Once you've identified your gift, the next step is to understand your purpose. Your purpose is how you use your gift to contribute to the world. It's the driving force that keeps you motivated and focused, even in the face of challenges. My purpose became clear through my struggles and triumphs. The rejection I faced in sports fueled my passion for gender equality and empowerment. My experiences in nursing and the corporate world highlighted the importance of authenticity and the need to create spaces where others could thrive.

To find your purpose, reflect on your personal history and the challenges you've overcome. These experiences often hold the key to understanding the problems you are uniquely equipped to solve. For instance, if you've faced adversity in a particular area, you might feel called to help others navigate similar challenges. Your purpose gives your life direction and meaning, transforming your gift into a powerful tool for positive change.

Path: Navigating Your Unique Journey

The final element of the Genius Identity Code™ is your path—the unique way you express your gift and fulfill your purpose. Your path is shaped by your personality, values, and life experiences. It's the journey that only you can undertake, marked by the distinctive way you navigate life's challenges and opportunities.

For me, the path included combining my medical background with my passion for art and coaching. It meant creating a business that not only supported my financial needs but also aligned with my values and aspirations. It's important to remember that your path is not a straight line; it's a dynamic and evolving journey that requires constant self-reflection and adjustment.

Focus: The Art of Staying Aligned

Focus is the ability to direct your attention and energy towards your goals, despite distractions and obstacles. It's the discipline to stay aligned with your gift, purpose, and path, even when life throws curveballs. Achieving focus requires clarity of vision and a deep commitment to your values and goals.

One of the most effective ways to maintain focus is through daily practices that reinforce your alignment. This can include setting clear intentions, creating actionable plans, and regularly reviewing your progress. For example, I start each day by reconnecting with my purpose and setting specific, achievable goals that move me closer to my vision. This practice helps me stay grounded and motivated, even when faced with challenges.

Working with Others: The Power of Collaboration

Achieving alignment and focus is not a solitary endeavor. Collaboration and support from others are crucial components of success. Surrounding yourself with a tribe of like-minded individuals who understand and support your journey can provide invaluable encouragement and guidance.

In my coaching practice, I emphasize the importance of building a strong support network. This includes finding mentors, peers, and allies who can offer insights, feedback, and emotional support. Working with others also means being open to diverse perspectives and ideas, which can enhance your creativity and problem-solving abilities.

Overcoming Your Goliaths

Every journey toward focus and alignment will encounter its own Goliaths—those seemingly insurmountable obstacles that test your resolve and strength. Overcoming these challenges requires a combination of resilience, resourcefulness, and support from others. Reflecting on my own experiences, I've learned that facing Goliaths head-on is not just about defeating them but also about learning and growing from the process.

For instance, my struggle with self-expression and authenticity in professional spaces taught me the importance of setting boundaries and finding my voice. Each challenge I faced, from navigating family dynamics to launching my coaching business, was a lesson in perseverance and self-belief.

Practical Steps to Focus and Align Your Life

To help you on your journey towards focus and alignment, here are some practical steps you can implement:

1. Identify Your Gift: Take time to reflect on your strengths and passions. Ask for feedback from those who know you well to gain insights into your unique abilities.

2. Define Your Purpose: Look back on your life experiences and identify the common themes and challenges you've overcome. Use these insights to understand your purpose and how you can contribute to the world.

3. Chart Your Path: Create a roadmap for your journey, outlining the steps you need to take to align your life with your gift and purpose. Be flexible and open to adjusting your path as you grow and evolve.

4. Cultivate Focus: Develop daily habits and practices that help you stay aligned with your goals. This can include setting intentions, creating actionable plans, and regularly reviewing your progress.

5. Build Your Tribe: Surround yourself with supportive and like-minded individuals who can offer encouragement, guidance, and diverse perspectives. Seek out mentors, peers, and allies who share your values and aspirations.

6. Embrace Resilience: Recognize that challenges and setbacks are a natural part of the journey. Use these experiences as opportunities for growth and learning. Stay committed to your vision, even when faced with obstacles.

7. Celebrate Your Wins: Take time to acknowledge and celebrate your achievements, no matter how small. Celebrating your successes can boost your motivation and reinforce your commitment to your goals.

Your Journey of Focus and Alignment

The journey of focus and alignment is a continuous process of self-discovery, growth, and empowerment. By embracing your unique gift, understanding your purpose, and navigating your path with clarity and determination, you can create a life that is truly aligned with your values and aspirations.

Remember, you are not alone on this journey. Seek support, collaborate with others, and stay resilient in the face of challenges. As you conquer your Goliaths, you will inspire others to do the same, contributing to a world where everyone can live authentically and fulfill their true potential.

STEPH SHINABERY

About Steph Shinabery: Steph Shinabery is The World's Best Possibility Coach, and a Nurse Anesthesiologist, Artist, Speaker, and the Founder of GENIUS CODE ACADEMY.

After spending much of her life in a career that lacked the inspiration and fulfillment she knew was available to her, she began a journey to answer the question: "What is it I truly desire?"

Her journey led to the creation of the Genius Identity Code™, a process for unlocking your gift, purpose and path, and helping people see, believe and execute their unique genius to achieve miraculous outcomes.

Steph works with creative experts, entrepreneurs and coaches to help them embrace their authenticity and create a life that gets them excited to jump out of bed every day!

You can find her talk, "Wake Up Your Genius Machine" on Amazon Prime Video's Speak Up: Empower Your Ideas, Season 4.

Author's Website: *www.StephShinabery.com* & *www.GeniusCodeAcademy.com*

Book Series Website: *www.ThePrinciplesOfDebbieAndGoliath.com*

"

You must learn to be still in
the midst of activity and to be
vibrantly alive in repose."

"

~ Indira Gandhi

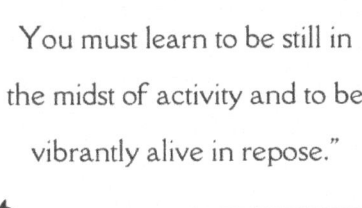

TAMMY THACKER

EMPOWERING THE NEXT GENERATION

Transitioning from a career in law enforcement to becoming an entrepreneur has been an incredible journey, but it's only part of my story. As I reflect on my experiences, I've realized the importance of focus and alignment in achieving my goals and empowering others, especially young women. This chapter is dedicated to sharing the lessons I've learned about maintaining focus, aligning my actions with my values, and working with others to create powerful synergies.

The Power of Focus

One of the most critical aspects of my journey has been learning to focus on what truly matters. In law enforcement, focus was not just a skill; it was a necessity. Every decision had to be precise and well-considered, especially when dealing with sensitive cases involving children. My commitment to making Heber City a safer place for children drove me to focus relentlessly on my responsibilities.

When I first became an officer, I faced numerous challenges. Being a female in a male-dominated field required an extra level of determination and focus. I had to prove myself continually, not only to my colleagues but also to the community. There were days when self-doubt crept in, but I reminded myself of my purpose. My focus on protecting and advocating for children in my community kept me going, even when the going got tough.

Alignment with Core Values

Throughout my career, I have aligned my actions with my core values of service, integrity, and compassion. This alignment has been the cornerstone of my professional and personal success. When I decided to transition to entrepreneurship, these values guided my choice of venture. Black Rifle Coffee's mission to support the military and first responders resonated deeply with me, as it mirrored my commitment to service.

Aligning my new career with my core values has been a rewarding experience. At Black Rifle Coffee, I have the opportunity to continue serving my community in a different capacity. This alignment ensures that my work remains meaningful and fulfilling, allowing me to stay motivated and passionate about what I do.

Trust and Faith

Trust and faith have been integral to my journey. In law enforcement, I had to trust my instincts and the training I received. There were countless situations where quick decisions were necessary, and trust in my abilities was crucial. Similarly, faith played a significant role in my daily life. Each shift began with a prayer for strength and guidance, helping me navigate the complexities of my job.

Trusting in a higher power and having faith in the process has helped me overcome numerous obstacles. It allowed me to remain calm and focused, even in the most challenging situations. This trust and faith have also been vital in my transition to entrepreneurship, giving me the confidence to take on new challenges and pursue my goals with determination.

Empowering the Next Generation

One of my greatest passions is empowering the next generation, particularly young women. Throughout my career, I've seen the importance of strong female role models. I strive to be a source of inspiration and support for young girls, showing them that they can achieve anything they set their minds to.

In Heber City, I initiated programs like Shop with a Cop and Kid's Academy to build stronger relationships between children and law enforcement. These programs have been instrumental in fostering trust and understanding. Seeing the impact these initiatives have had on the children involved has been incredibly fulfilling. It's a reminder that empowering others starts with small, meaningful actions.

Building Synergies through Collaboration

Collaboration and teamwork have been crucial in both my law enforcement and entrepreneurial careers. In law enforcement, working closely with colleagues and community members was essential to achieving our goals. As an entrepreneur, I've found that collaboration with my business partners and community leaders has been key to our success at Black Rifle Coffee.

One of the most rewarding aspects of my work has been the ability to create synergies with others. For example, partnering with local schools and organizations to support community initiatives has allowed us to make a more significant impact. By aligning our efforts and working together, we've been able to achieve more than we could individually.

Overcoming Real-Life Goliaths

Throughout my life, I've faced numerous "Goliaths"—significant challenges that seemed insurmountable at the time. Each of these challenges has taught me valuable lessons about resilience, perseverance, and the importance of staying true to my values.

One of the most profound challenges was overcoming the prejudices and biases I encountered as a female officer. It wasn't easy, and there were times when I questioned my path. However, I learned to focus on what I could control: my actions, my attitude, and my dedication to my work.

By staying aligned with my values and maintaining a clear focus, I was able to overcome these obstacles and prove myself in my field.

Another significant challenge was the transition to entrepreneurship. Leaving a stable career in law enforcement to start a new venture was daunting. However, my focus on service and my commitment to my values guided me through the transition. Trusting in my abilities and having faith in the process helped me navigate this new path and find success.

Inspiring Young Women to Achieve Their Goals

My journey has been filled with lessons that I hope to pass on to young women aspiring to achieve their goals. Here are some key takeaways:

1. Believe in Yourself: Confidence is crucial. Trust your abilities and believe in your potential. Don't let self-doubt or external negativity deter you from pursuing your dreams.

2. Stay Focused: Focus on what truly matters to you. Align your actions with your goals and values, and stay committed to your path, even when faced with challenges.

3. Seek Support: Surround yourself with supportive people who believe in you. A strong support system can provide the encouragement and strength needed to overcome obstacles.

4. Embrace Service: Find ways to serve others. Serving your community not only makes a positive impact but also provides a sense of fulfillment and purpose.

5. Foster Collaboration: Work with others to achieve common goals. Collaboration and teamwork can create powerful synergies that lead to greater success.

6. Trust and Faith: Trust in yourself and have faith in the process. Trusting your instincts and having faith in a higher power can guide you through difficult times and help you stay focused on your goals.

As I continue my journey, I remain committed to empowering others, particularly young women. My story is a testament to the power of focus, alignment, and collaboration. By staying true to our values and working together, we can overcome any challenge and achieve our goals.

I encourage young women to take the lessons from my journey and apply them to their own lives. Believe in yourself, stay focused, seek support, embrace service, foster collaboration, and trust in the process. These principles will guide you in overcoming your own Goliaths and achieving your dreams.

Reflecting on my journey, I'm grateful for the opportunities and experiences that have shaped me. From my early days in law enforcement to my current role as an entrepreneur, each step has taught me valuable lessons about focus, alignment, and the power of collaboration.

My story is one of perseverance, faith, and a commitment to making a positive impact. I've faced many challenges, but each one has made me stronger and more determined. By believing in myself, staying focused on my goals, and working with others, I've been able to achieve more than I ever imagined.

As I look to the future, I'm excited to continue this journey and inspire others to pursue their dreams. Together, we can create a world where young women feel empowered to achieve their goals and make a difference in their communities.

Thank you for joining me on this journey. I hope my story inspires you to stay focused, aligned with your values, and committed to making a positive impact. Remember, we all have the power to overcome our Goliaths and achieve greatness. Believe in yourself, trust the process, and never underestimate the power of focus and alignment.

TAMMY THACKER

About Tammy Thacker: Tammy Thacker, a distinguished figure in Heber City, Utah, epitomizes the blend of dedication to public service and entrepreneurial spirit. Raised in Heber City, Tammy's journey began at Wasatch High School, where she laid the foundations of her commitment to her community.

Tammy's career in law enforcement, marked by tenures at both the Heber City Police Department and the Wasatch County Sheriff's Office, reflects her unwavering commitment to public safety and community wellbeing. Her time in local law enforcement not only allowed her to serve her community but also provided her with invaluable experiences that shaped her leadership and organizational skills.

Transitioning from law enforcement to the business world, Tammy embarked on a new venture as the leader of Black Rifle Coffee in Heber City. This entrepreneurial leap showcases her versatile skill set and her ability to adapt and thrive in diverse environments. At Black Rifle Coffee, she combines her deep understanding of the local community with her leadership abilities, steering the company towards growth while maintaining its core values.

Amidst her professional endeavors, Tammy remains deeply rooted in her community and family life in Heber City. Her story is a testament to her resilience, adaptability, and enduring commitment to her hometown.

Author's Website: *www.BlackRifleCoffee.com*

Book Series Website: *www.ThePrinciplesOfDebbieAndGoliath.com*

TASHA SMITH

THE TOOLS TO BEAT GOLIATH

In my life, there have been many times when I had to face a Goliath or have had Goliath situations. When these moments were presented to me, I was very scared and sometimes confused about what I should do and how I should handle it. Sometimes, I was fortunate enough to have a moment to think and figure out how to tackle the situation. However, other times I had to think on my feet.

Fortunately, I was raised on a solid foundation. By no means am I trying to say that I did not experience hardships and disappointment. I was taught to do my best and figure out the lessons that were being taught in that moment from those disappointing times. When necessary, use the lessons that I learned later to my advantage. In life, if you are fortunate enough, you have or had parents or guardians to teach you right from wrong at an early age. Also, if you are lucky, they would have equipped you with the additional proper tools for you to set out in life to be successful.

My personal belief is that if you put your mind to it, you can conquer any Goliath. Growing up and traveling through life there was always a part of me that truly believed that. I had just to figure out how to do it. When my parents started to release me into the hypothetical wild, also known as the world, they made sure I always carried my 5 theoretical stones in my bag just like David, or as I like to call them, my beliefs. Each one of my 5 beliefs had a name, love, self-worth, faith, trust, and courage.

The first stone in my belief bag is part of a duo. This duo is called love and self-worth. I was taught that I must love myself like no other. You cannot love anyone else until you first love yourself. I strongly believe that everyone should engage in being in a personal relationship with themselves. Take some time, date yourself and get to know you, so you can fall in love with yourself. I know some of you that are reading this may be saying to yourself that I am crazy. To all of you that are thinking that, you are partially correct. I am crazy but crazy in love with myself.

The second half of the duo is called self-worth. In order to arrive at this point, you have to first discover and fall in love with yourself. A simple definition of self-worth is that you value yourself. There are so many of us walking around the world without having self-worth. If you do not know your value others will treat you any way that they feel in any moment. Most of the time that treatment is not nice and less than par. When you discover your worth, you will feel different and will not accept any treatment that you feel is beneath you. Not only will you feel different the world will notice the difference in you as well. What they will see is confidence. You will not be afraid to ask for what you want. Also, if you do not get it, you will not be afraid to say thanks but no thanks and keep it moving.

It was very important to me to start off with my power duo because in my opinion they are two of the most important beliefs. Without those two everything else would be extremely difficult to achieve. It takes some time and patience to get to these destinations. However, once you arrive you will not leave. Also, you cannot expect others to love and value you if you do not love and value yourself. Until these lessons are comprehended you will have issues within yourself.

The third stone in my belief bag is called faith. My simple meaning of faith is to believe or trust in what you can or cannot see. I have faith in God and the universe. I believe with God, all things are possible. As long as you have God, you will never walk alone. Sometimes, we feel lonely and feel as if we are going through everything by ourselves. We feel that way because at the end of the day we are human. But, as long as we have faith, we will always remember that we are never alone in our journey. My faith in the universe is just as strong. I believe the universe is like a gift that keeps giving. It has no favorites and you get out of it what you put into it. The actions and words that we put out into it always has a way of seeking and finding us in some way, shape or form.

The fourth stone in my bag is trust. In this world it is sometimes very hard to trust others. Trust is something that has to be earned and takes time to get comfortable with. The person that we have to have trust in first is ourselves. We have to believe that we can trust ourselves enough to make sound judgements and decisions for our life. There always comes a time in our life when we must learn to trust someone other than ourselves. We were not created to walk the earth completely alone. We all need help at some point in our lives for various reasons. When that time comes, we must trust ourselves enough to make the right judgement or decision to put trust in someone else.

The final stone in my belief bag is courage. The meaning of courage is the ability to do something that frightens you. Having the strength to be courageous can be extremely scary and nerve-racking. To be successful in life we have to sometimes step out of our comfort zones and forge ahead. Do not focus on the fact that you may feel intimidated by someone or something. You have to build up enough courage in yourself and concentrate on the goal that you are trying to achieve. Think of the journey like a video game. The obstacles are coins that you must collect along the path to unlock your ultimate winning power, called the goal.

Since I have used all of the stones in my belief bag, I am a stronger and more complete person. I do not have to rely on any other person to make me feel complete or happy. Now I can help and love others, being my best self. I am more than equipped to battle any Goliath that crosses my path!

Dedication: This chapter is dedicated to all of you who did not know that you needed to hear what I said until after you read it!

TASHA SMITH

About Tasha Smith: Tasha is a resident of North Carolina by way of New York. She is a mom of four and loves spending quality time with her family. In her spare time, Tasha creates various DIY crafts and interior design projects. Her favorite kind of entertainment is attending concerts, plays, and comedy shows. In the future, one of Tasha's greatest aspirations is to help provide shelter and assistance to those who are in need and less fortunate.

Book Series Website: *www.ThePrinciplesOfDebbieAndGoliath.com*

TAYLOR L. COLE

CONFIDENTLY CREATED ON PURPOSE FOR A PURPOSE

If I'd known you were coming, I'd have baked a cake!

I have a vivid memory from when I was about 3 or 4 years old, spending a summer afternoon at my grandma Mamma Fannie's house. She often sang hymns while going about her chores. She was always giving me creative projects to complete and on this particular day, she handed me some alphabet letters (some were from a toy store, and some were letters she cut out from cardboard cereal and cracker boxes), a notebook, and markers, and encouraged me to spell words, write sentences, and color in the notebook.

Despite already being up and working since before 5AM, my grandma managed to prepare breakfast, collect eggs from the hen house, do laundry (using a clothesline for the sheets and blankets), wash dishes by hand, dust the furniture, sweep, and vacuum the house, and who knows what else! I pitched in and helped where I could, but I was fully engaged in my art and spelling project. The house was spotless and smelled of freshly baked lemon cake.

Lost in my creativity, I was interrupted by the doorbell and the creak of the screen door opening. A familiar voice exclaimed excitedly, "We're here! We're here!" My grandma rushed to the door, beaming with joy, "I knew it! Welcome! We've been expecting you!" The voice belonged to my great-aunt, who responded in surprise, "Expecting us? Who told you we were coming? It was supposed to be a surprise!" Undeterred, my grandma smiled warmly and replied, "I'm always ready for a visit from my sweet sister."

This regularly happened at my grandma and grandpa's house. Not only was my grandma ready at any given time for visitors, but she also kept a cake baked just in case! She was always ready for guests. She expected them and she celebrated their arrival. She also knew that her sister loved lemon cake and baked it because she wanted to have something special on hand that she liked.

The same is true for us with God. In the Bible, Jeremiah 1:5 says, "I knew you before I formed you in your mother's womb. Before you were born I set you apart…" Just like for Jeremiah, as children of God, He knows each of us. He knew us before we were born, and He celebrates when we invite him into our daily lives. He welcomes us to fellowship with Him and the invitation is always open.

Self-help books and social media videos often suggest that you try to discover the meaning and purpose for your life by getting in touch with yourself and knowing your truth. But that's the wrong place to start.

God, the Creator of Heaven, Earth, and all things thought about you, long before you were born. God's preplanning for your unmatched life was thorough, complete, and purposeful.

He contemplated who you would become and how He would be able to use you, making a list of all the people who would be impacted by your influence. He sees great potential in you, and you should always remember that. You are who you are by divine design and eternal calling.

Don't underestimate your gifts, talents, interests, and deepest desires. You were created under God's authority and supervision, with every aspect of your being crafted with love and attention to detail.

When you entered the stage of history, it wasn't a random event. God created you with the same care and value as the first humans on earth,

Adam and Eve. You were fashioned in God's heart for this moment in time.

Purposefully on Purpose

Knowing that God anticipated you, has plans for you and that you were created on purpose for a purpose should give you energy and curiosity. The first time someone told me that I was created with a purpose, I had lots of questions. "What is my purpose? How can I fulfill it? Is it random? How much control over my purpose do I have?" I remember talking to friends, family, teachers, mentors, and about anyone who would indulge me. I'm so grateful that my grandparents, parents, and countless relatives and friends consistently reminded me of some core truths that helped me and I know these truths will help you, too.

Your true identity and purpose come from Jesus Christ.

God is good and He's so good to you that He created you with love for a purpose, on purpose.

You are significant and part of a bigger plan that was set in motion long before you were born.

Yet even with those core truths embedded in my mind, I still pondered questions like, "What if I miss my purpose? How much of my purpose is tied to my education, occupation, and familial status?" Finally, I found an exceptional book by Rick Warren titled, *The Purpose-Driven Life.* I read it from cover to cover, then I purchased the study guide and bought a dozen copies to give to those same family members, friends, teachers, and mentors. Rick Warren says there are five benefits to living a purpose-driven life:

Knowing your purpose gives meaning to your life. We were made to have meaning. When life has meaning, you can bear almost anything; without it, nothing is bearable. Without God, life has no purpose, and without purpose, life has no meaning. Without meaning, life has no significance or hope. Hope is essential to your life.

Knowing your purpose simplifies your life. It defines what you do and what you don't do. Your purpose becomes the standard you use to evaluate which activities are essential and which aren't. Without a clear purpose, you have no foundation on which you base decisions, allocate your time, and use your resources. You will tend to make choices based on circumstances, pressures, and your mood at that moment.

Knowing your purpose focuses your life. It concentrates your effort and energy on what's important. You become effective at being selective.

Knowing your purpose motivates your life. Purpose always produces passion. Nothing energizes like a clear purpose. On the other hand, passion dissipates when you lack purpose.

Knowing your purpose prepares you for eternity. Many people spend their lives trying to create a lasting legacy on earth. They want to be remembered when they're gone. Yet what ultimately matters most will not be what others say about your life, but what God says. Living to create an earthly legacy is a short-sighted goal. A wiser use of time is to build an eternal, Kingdom legacy.

Consider the significance of God choosing to place your life on earth now, so that you would seek Him wholeheartedly and share His goodness with others. This is a profound purpose that should never be overlooked or minimized. You are here to discover who God is and to share that discovery with those around you. There is no greater reason to live than that!

Worldly Existence vs. God's Kingdom Purpose

The world would have you to believe that you should focus on yourself, your needs, and the things you want. A worldly view of purpose is heavily centered on your career, material possessions, pleasures, approvals, accolades, and social media likes, followers, and fans. While these things can bring satisfaction, they're only temporary.

I remember in the 6th grade I was training to compete in a track meet. I practiced every afternoon during the week and on Saturdays. My parents would time me and I'd list my best times on a dry erase board in the kitchen. Although I enjoyed running track, if I was truly honest, I enjoyed competing (and winning) against our rival town even more. My motivation for running track was the medals and recognition I would receive and the opportunity to brag that I helped my team beat our neighboring rival. I, in fact, won track meets and our team often beat our rivals.

Not long ago, I was in the attic at my house and opened a dusty photo album that was tucked away in a storage bin. There were dozens of medals, ribbons, and photos of me in uniform for cheerleading, softball, basketball, and track. These once-coveted awards now felt like distant yet cherished memories. Over time, the accolades that I craved became less important, and forgotten.

There's nothing wrong with striving for excellence in sports, academics, your career, or other activities. However, allowing these pursuits to define your identity falls short of God's best for your life. What you do according to worldly standards and why you were created by God for His Kingdom purpose are two different things. Worldly aspirations weaken your potential, but the most reassuring news for anyone facing a weakened or insecure life is this: God, your Creator, is by your side, and He is with you. You don't need to prove yourself, achieve greatness, or have credentials when you have the Lord with you. All He asks is for you to accept His will and plan. The Lord promised to be with Jeremiah, and He promises to be with you, too!

What steps can you take today to recognize your God-given purpose? Where's an area where you can stop thinking of things of the world and instead think about God's Kingdom purpose for your life?

Spend some time in prayer asking God to show you how you were created to fit into His perfect plan. All you have to do is have an open, honest conversation with God and ask Him to reveal His purpose for your life, then wait and listen for His voice. You are fearfully and wonderfully made. You were made on purpose for a purpose!

Are you ready to confidently step into your purpose? Let's connect.

TAYLOR L. COLE

About Taylor L. Cole: Taylor L. Cole is a seasoned professional dedicated to helping meaningful brands capture the attention they deserve. With a career spanning over 14 years, Taylor has honed her skills in Communications, PR, and social media, working with Fortune 500 companies, multi-national corporations, and startups across various industries including travel, tech, healthcare, and consumer products.

Starting her journey in the world of television while still in high school, Taylor quickly made her mark, producing her first major show as an undergraduate at Southern Methodist University. She has since taken on leadership roles in communications and public relations at renowned companies such as Kimberly Clark, Hotels.com, Expedia, and Sabre.

Taylor's extensive experience has allowed her to work with a diverse range of business owners, entertainers, and travel suppliers, teaching her the crucial lesson that brands must captivate their audience with the right marketing exposure to avoid falling into obscurity.

As a guide for brands and leaders, Taylor specializes in crafting effective messaging and on-camera strategies, featuring her clients on quality, international TV programs and podcasts. She is the executive producer and host of *"The Focus"* and *"Speak Up"* on Amazon Prime Video, as well as the travel TV show *"Hotel Hunt,"* where she explores stunning destinations and uncovers unique accommodations. Her latest project is *"Workable Faith,"* a show where she engages with business leaders about integrating faith into the marketplace. Taylor is also a dedicated community member, serving on various non-profit boards, business leadership groups, and actively participating in her church. Her involvement includes roles with the American Diabetes Association, Fellowship Power Lunch, Truth at Work, Valley Creek Church, and SMU.

She invites brands ready to step into the spotlight to connect with her at TVwithTLC.com, where they can embark on a journey to refine their messaging, identify their key audience, and build the perfect platform to share their unique voice. Taylor's specialties encompass a wide range of services including being a Brand Spokesperson, TV Host for Travel & Lifestyle Products, TV Production, Podcasting, Christian Businesses and Values-Based Initiatives, Author & Professional Speaker Visibility, Strategic Public Relations, Marketing Consulting, Communications Strategy, Media Coaching & Training, and serving as a Fractional Communications & PR Executive. She is the proven fixer that brands need to shine in their respective industries.

Author's Website: *www.TVWithTLC.com*

Book Series Website: *www.ThePrinciplesOfDebbieAndGoliath.com*

TLC

VIKKI ROOD

TO THINE OWN SELF BE IN ALIGNMENT

"You are so sensitive, Vikki. You are so dramatic. Why do you take things so personally? You are being too much."

These are things that I used to think defined me. Maybe it's because I'm a Cancer, maybe it's because I grew up in an alcoholic home. It doesn't really matter, does it?

What I have discovered is that, when I focused on those things, when I was a victim of my circumstances, I believed that was just how I was. I thought my life had to simply work around my moods, my ups and downs. That people didn't understand me, and I simply had to go at it alone.

When I was 15, I found that drinking gave me freedom from that overthinking. I felt like I fit in. I was funnier and much cooler. And that lasted and worked for me for many years—until then it didn't.

At 12 years old, at my 6th-grade camping field trip, it was the first time I wanted to hit the eject button. I remember holding my pin—those were the days when you wore pins on your jean jackets—and thinking, what would it matter if I slit my wrist and just never went home? Those thoughts continued into my 20s and escalated in my 30s when I actually tried to end it all in a blackout.

However, instead, I decided to get help. I had been going to therapy for 10 years and, of course, never shared the truth about my dark thoughts or how much I drank. I was diagnosed with major depressive disorder.

Until one day, I was walking down the hallway, looked into my kids' room, and thought, I don't want to screw up their lives, but I don't have any clue how to stop feeling this way. Because honestly, drinking and drugs were the only things that allowed me to pause the pain of being me. It was hard, ugly, and humiliating. As a mother, I have two beautiful humans that I get to share this life with, and the fact that I have learned how to choose me has made a huge impact on my ability to be present with them in my life.

I decided in that moment that I was going to try to get help. And I did. I started to get honest with my psychologist, my therapist, and myself. I had a sister who was in a twelve-step group and I asked her to take me to a meeting. That was 14 years ago, and I am so grateful for the courage I had in those moments of desperation.

What has transpired in these 14 years has been nothing short of an absolute miracle. I have always been a student of personal development. Of course, during the years prior to living a sober life in recovery, it didn't have any lasting results, neither did the antidepressants.

However, working the 12 steps was an absolute catalyst for my healing journey. And here's what I have learned about myself since then: Life is a beautiful, wonderful, messy, magical, and epic adventure. We each have our own way of being, and what I have learned in recent years is that being emotional, passionate, and loving is my strength, and when I use it for my own healing and growth, I am able to be of service to others in a healthy way.

Something that I hear a lot at 12-step meetings is "To thine own self be true." This is from Hamlet by William Shakespeare. It is a truth with a capital T. You see, finding alignment within myself has created this new and miraculous life I now get to live.

It's not perfect by any means, but today, when I am out in the world, I check in with myself. I have a new set of principles which I had no idea were things you could really live by. I thought everyone was full of it. But today, I keep my word to myself. I live with honesty, and before, for some reason, I thought that honesty was just about what you did for and with others.

The honesty that I'm talking about here is with myself. You see, I was a person always trying to keep everyone around me happy. Growing up, I was the natural caregiver and always wanted to keep the peace. My habit of putting others before me took over my every day. When I got sober, it was an opportunity to know myself, to discover myself, and to show through action that I matter just as much as all those around me.

Learning how to ask for what I needed wasn't an easy task. But today, I can say what it is that I prefer, and what it is that brings me joy and support. It was baby steps separating myself from the feelings of others. This is the key. I can coexist with those I love while staying true to myself. I don't have to go along to get along. I don't have to hide my emotions. And, go figure, my emotions aren't so up and down. There is peace in my heart.

What it all boils down to is that I am in alignment with myself today. I can recognize where I am going and what it is that I am willing to shift to create a life that is loving, kind, and compassionate to myself and others.

When I learned how much easier it is to live in this world when I share my thoughts, feelings, and truth, my focus and direction shifted toward being the best version of myself, and that changed. When my son was in 2nd grade, we found out that he had ADHD and dyslexia. Because of my focus and commitment to my own growth, I was able to be there for him, take a stand for him at school, and even go two days per week for reading tutoring. I was able to be committed to him and provide him with the support he needed without allowing my feelings to take over.

Here are the guiding forces that I choose to live my life by, and when I keep my focus on these things, success, love, peace, and joyful living are evident and attainable:

- Love is my guiding light.
- Honesty with myself and others.
- Connection with what my body is telling me.
- Kindness in all that I do.
- Gratitude for what I have and who I am, and gratitude for all the humans in my life.
- Compassion for all.
- What I practice grows stronger!

What me and my good friends practice is radical honesty, and what I choose to do is ask for the support I need. If something comes up and I need to process it verbally, I communicate that I'm not looking for advice, or if I want their thoughts, I ask for feedback. I've also discovered that asking others what they need keeps the authenticity and compassion in the relationship in a healthy way!

VIKKI ROOD

About Vikki Rood: Vikki Rood is a passionate advocate for joyful living, a seasoned empowerment coach, and a published author dedicated to helping individuals uncover their authentic selves and live lives filled with purpose, empowerment, and boundless joy. Vikki invites you to join her on a journey of self-discovery, empowerment, and joy.

Through coaching, workshops, and a thriving community, she'll help you uncover your authentic self, embrace your unique path, and find fulfillment in every facet of your life.

Author's Website: *www.VikkiRoodCoaching.com*

Book Series Website: *www.ThePrinciplesOfDebbieAndGoliath.com*

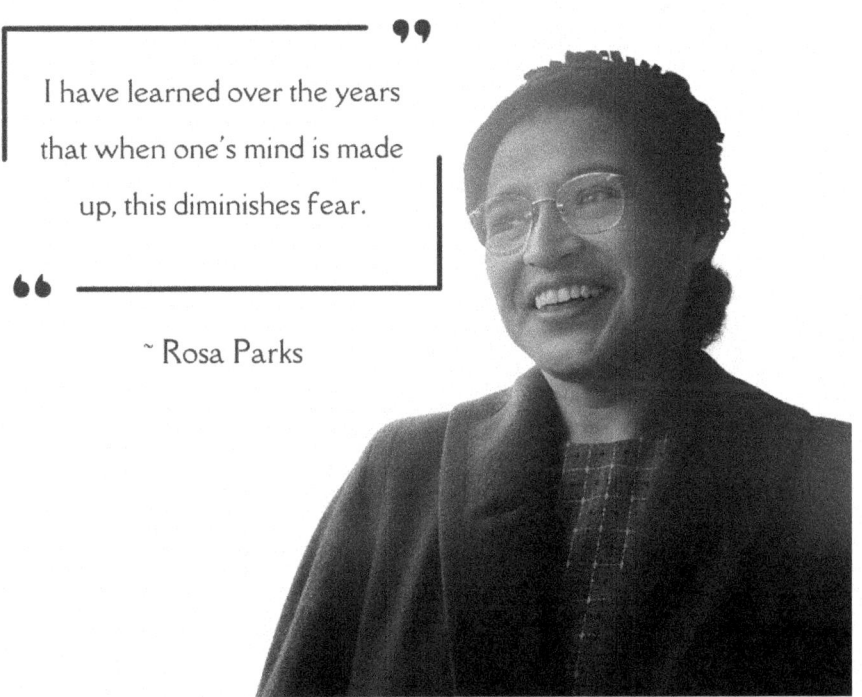

> I have learned over the years that when one's mind is made up, this diminishes fear.

~ Rosa Parks

FEMALE EMPOWERMENT RESOURCES

THE PRINCIPLES OF DEBBIE & GOLIATH

In the journey of empowerment and overcoming challenges, it's crucial to have access to resources and support, especially in areas that profoundly affect women's lives. *While The Principles of Debbie and Goliath* book series is an inspiration and blueprint, we recognize the importance of direct support and advocacy. We highlight below some key resources:

Domestic Violence & Trafficking

* **Unsilenced Voices** [www.unsilencedvoices.org]: Unsilenced Voices (UV) is a global 501(c)3 nonprofit that empowers survivors of domestic violence, sexual assault, and human trafficking in multiple countries through advocacy, education, and support services.

* **National Domestic Violence Hotline** [www.thehotline.org]: This vital resource provides confidential support to victims of domestic violence and trafficking. They offer a 24/7 hotline, emergency services, and a wealth of information for those seeking help.

* **Rape, Abuse & Incest National Network** [www.rainn.org]: The nation's largest anti-sexual violence organization, RAINN operates the National Sexual Assault Hotline and carries out programs to prevent sexual violence, help survivors, and ensure that perpetrators are brought to justice.

* **The Slave Free Project** [www.slavefreeproject.com]: The Slave Free Project is building awareness and equipping others to prevent and fight human trafficking, breaking the silence and uniting communities to create the change the world has been waiting for.

* **Court Appointed Special Advocates** [www.nationalcasagal.org]: The National CASA/GAL Association for Children supports a network of 939 state CASA/GAL organizations and local CASA/

GAL programs operating in 49 states (all but North Dakota) and the District of Columbia.

Female Financial Literacy

- **National Endowment for Financial Education (NEFE)** [www.nefe.org]: NEFE is a nonprofit dedicated to improving financial literacy and effectiveness among all Americans. They provide a wealth of educational resources, research, and tools to empower women to make informed financial decisions.

- **Smart About Money** [www.smartaboutmoney.org]: A program of NEFE, this resource offers free courses and tools on a range of financial topics, from budgeting to saving for retirement, tailored to help women gain financial independence and literacy.

- **Women's Institute for Financial Education** [www.wife.org]: WIFE focuses specifically on empowering women with financial education. They offer seminars, workshops, and a variety of resources aimed at increasing financial knowledge and independence among women.

- **Napoleon Hill Foundation** [www.naphill.org]: The Napoleon Hill Foundation is a nonprofit educational institution dedicated to making the world a better place in which to live.

Military Family Support for Females

- **National Military Family Association** [www.militaryfamily.org]: This organization focuses on supporting military families through comprehensive programs such as spouse scholarships, child education initiatives, and wellness activities, with particular attention to the unique needs of female family members.

- **Blue Star Families** [www.bluestarfam.org]: Blue Star Families offers a range of support services, including career development, caregiving, and family support, specifically tailored to address the challenges faced by military spouses and female family members.

- **Service Women's Action Network** [www.servicewomen.org]: SWAN is dedicated to supporting, connecting, and advocating for servicewomen and female veterans. They offer resources, peer support, and advocacy for issues including gender discrimination and military sexual trauma.

- **Center For Women Vets** [www.va.gov/womenvet/]: The Center for Women Veterans' (CWV) mission is to monitor and coordinate VA's administration of health care, benefits, services, and programs for women Veterans. We serve as an advocate for cultural transformation and to raise awareness of the responsibility to treat women Veterans with dignity and respect to #BringWomenVeteransHome2VA.

Additional Resources

- **World Youth Horizons** [www.worldyouthhorizons.com]: World Youth Horizons is a 501(c)(3)global non-profit organization that provides support to youth around the world by providing food, shelter, education, and experiences to help improve their economic conditions and to encourage youth to expand their horizons.

- **Unstoppable Foundation** [www.unstoppablefoundation.org]: The Unstoppable Foundation is a non-profit humanitarian organization bringing sustainable education to children and communities in developing countries thereby creating a safer and more just world for everyone. Their Mission: To ensure EVERY child has access to the life-long gift of an education.

- **Broadway Hearts** [www.broadwayhearts.org]: Broadway Hearts is a not-for-profit organization bringing professional Broadway performers, music, and joy to the extraordinary kids in treatment at children's hospitals nationwide.

- **God's Bucket Brigade** [www.godsbucketbrigade.org]: Blessing and loving the homeless and less fortunate with help for today, and hope for tomorrow.

- **Seek Her Foundation** [www.seekher.org]: SeekHer Foundation is on a mission to bridge the gender gap in mental health through advocacy, research, and support for emerging leaders who are impacting change in their local communities and beyond.

- **Lindsey Vonn Foundation** [www.lindseyvonnfoundation.org]: Impacting student-age girls 10-18 from underserved U.S. communities with empowering self-esteem camps, and scholarships to participate in tech, sports and enrichment programs so that they can grow to be tomorrow's leaders and visionaries.

- **Girls Who Code** [www.girlswhocode.com]: Girls Who Code is a captivating after-school learning experience that introduces middle school and high school girls to computer science classes within a supportive sisterhood of peers. Thanks to rising women's tech events around the U.S. and woman-focused organizations, girls are becoming more and more exposed to careers in technology.

- **Girls Inc** [www.girlsinc.org]: In partnership with schools and at Girls Inc. centers, we focus on the development of the whole girl. She learns to value herself, take risks, and discover and develop her inherent strengths. The combination of long-lasting mentoring relationships, a pro-girl environment, and evidence-based programming equips girls to navigate gender, economic, and social barriers, and grow up healthy, educated, and independent.

- **Junior Habitude Warrior** [www.juniorhabitudewarrior.com]: Junior Habitude Warrior is an amazing organization providing strategies of growth for kids and teenagers focusing on building confidence, leadership, non-bullying, and personal development.

These organizations represent a beacon of hope and support for women facing these major issues. We encourage readers to utilize these resources and share them with those who might benefit from their services.

HABITUDE WARRIOR & INTEGRITY PUBLISHING EDITORIAL TEAM

Habitude Warrior International and Integrity Publishing take great pride in our editorial team who put their sweat, tears, and heart into each and every project and national bestseller! Thank you team!

JON KOVACH JR.
Team Manager

PAT MINTON
VP of Operations

JILLIAN KOVACH
Editorial Manager

Jon Kovach Jr. strives to assist every author and every team member in the process of self-development for ultimate success.

Pat Minton has been with the Habitude Warrior International team for over 20 years getting her start with Brian Tracy & Erik Swanson.

Jillian is a vital team member of Habitude Warrior & Integrity Publishing bringing her expertise managing our Editorial Department.

FATIMA HURD
Editorial Team & Photographer

LAUREN COBB
Editorial Team Member

Fatima is our Professional Photographer for Habitude Warrior as well as one of our members on the Proofing Department team.

Lauren Cobb is part of our Proofing Department for Habitude Warrior & Integrity Publishing as well as one of our authors.

To inquire about joining our team please send us an email to Team@HabitudeWarrior.com